Cruise Chooser

Buyer's Guide to Cruises:
Bargains, Discounts & Deals
How to Get the Best for Less.

Mary Fallon Miller

Every effort has been made to ensure the accuracy of information throughout this book. Dear Reader, please note that prices, programs and itineraries change. Verify information with your travel agent before making final travel plans.

Ticket to Adventure
PO Box 41005
St. Petersburg, FL 33743-1005
800-929-7447
editor@cruisechooser.com
www.cruisechooser.com

Copyright © 2001 by Mary Fallon Miller

Art Director: Randall Hall

All rights reserved. No part of this book may be reproduced or transmitted in any form or by any means, electronic or mechanical, including photocopying, recording, or by any information storage and retrieval system, without permission in writing from the publisher.

Media please contact Anne Wright:
1-800-929-7447   editor@cruisechooser.com

ISBN 0-9624019-2-7

CIP DATA
Miller, Mary Fallon, 1963-
    Cruise chooser : buyer's guide to cruises :
bargains, discounts & deals : how to get the
best for less / Mary Fallon Miller
        p.cm.
Includes bibliographical references and index.
ISBN 0-9624019-2-7 (pbk)
    1. Ocean travel. 2. Cruise ships. I. Title.

G550 .M55 2001
910'.2'02--dc21

00-044300

Cruise Chooser

Buyer's Guide to Cruises:
Bargains, Discounts & Deals
How to Get the Best for Less.

Why Cruise Chooser?

Are you ready for a **vacation**?
Thinking of taking a **cruise**?
Shopping for the perfect cruise **can be confusing - so many choices: ships - destinations - prices!** How do know you've got the **right cruise** for you? How can you make sure you get the **best price**? **Whether you're a savvy old salt or shopping for your first cruise - Cruise Chooser makes it easy.**

See Inside:

FUN Personality Quiz!
What's your vacation personality?

$500 Guarantee - Use Cruise Chooser and you will save money - *guaranteed*!

25 Ways You'll Save Money:
Tips on Bargains & Discounts make you the expert.

Top 40 Cruise Questions & Answers

Savings for *Solo Travelers, Babyboomers, Grandparents & Grandchildren, Families & Children, Mature Travelers, Honeymooners, Bargain Hunters ...*

How to get the Perfect Stateroom

Use the money-saving tips in Cruise Chooser and save $500 on your next uise vacation,

Guaranteed!

We're so confident in our Cruise Chooser $500 guarantee - we put it in writing:

If, after using Cruise Chooser's money-saving tips, you do not save $500 on your next cruise, Ticket to Adventure Publishing will refund the cost of your Cruise Chooser book in full.

Request your refund from:
Ticket to Adventure
PO Box 41005
St. Petersburg, FL 33743-1005

It's that simple! Get Cruise Chooser and Get the Best Cruise for Less.
Guaranteed!

How to Cruise like a VIP

50+ Cruise Line Profiles: ships, destinations...

Hot Trends in Cruising
   Tips for getting the perfect cruise for:
   Babyboomers, Grandparents, Bargain Hunters,
   Families & Children, Solo Travelers and more...

Health, Safety & Security for the whole family.

EASY CHECKLISTS
❑ What to Wear
❑ What to Pack
❑ Perfect Stateroom: Features, Convenience, Location
❑ Getting your Passport
❑ Honeymooners
❑ Mature Travelers
❑ Babies on board
❑ Children's Fun & Safety

New Cyberguide: Money-Saving Web Sites

Plus more resources: books, magazines, videos,
newsletters & specialty travel agencies to make your
cruise the best!

The first guide to put <u>you</u> first!

Get the Best for Less - Get Cruise Chooser!

Dedication

To Charles and Rini Miller

Acknowledgements

To my family:

Capt. Bill Miller and Sue, Amy and Jeff Miller.
Chris Miller and Connie, Maeve and Lorcan Miller.
Wishing the Millers a future that holds travel, adventure and romance.
Rini Miller for her unfailing love.
Don Andrus, whose mechanical wizardry is only exceeded by his generous heart,

Thanks to champions of the cause:

Janet Harris, Diana "When you going to get that book out" Smiles, Tommy Kelderhouse, Susan & Bongo Walsh, Katharine Dufais, Dutchie Meinsen, Bernie Feder, Patty Matheis, Timothy R. Tuthill, Tommy & Tracy Broncuccio, Randy "O great Randino" Hall, Kathy Marlor, National Association of Professional Martial Artists, Monday & Saturday Diners, Leslie Zane, Joy Lafray Little, Jerry and Chantall Gaudioso, The Postal Experts at Crossroads, Main and Euclid, Brian of Zephyrhills, The Mayor and Council of North Shore Park, Tierra Verde Swim Zone, Rangers of Ft. Desoto, Circle of Friends, Power Pals, the 7am.

Acknowledgements

Cruise Lines International Association, CLIA, **Jim Godsman, Bob Sharak, Ann Burquieres**; American Society of Travel Agents, ASTA, **Richard Copland, Cheryl Ahearn, Bill Connors**; Institute of Certified Travel Agents, ICTA, **Jack Mannix, Alexis Rochefort, Pat Gagnon**; National Association of Cruise Oriented Agents, NACOA, **Donna Esposito**; Association of Retail Travel Agents, ARTA, **John Hawks, Pat Funk**; Florida Caribbean Cruise Association, FCCA, American Classic Voyages Co. (American Hawaii Cruises, Delta Queen Coastal Cruises, Delta Queen Steamboat Co., United States Lines), **Lucette Brehm, Susan Oakland**; American West Steamboat; Bergen Line/Norwegian Coastal Voyages; Canyon Ranch at Sea; Carnival Cruise Lines, **Aly Bello, Jennifer de la Cruz**; Celebrity Cruises, **Elizabeth Jakeway, Tania Rodriguez**; Clipper Cruise Line, **Elizabeth McQuinn, Mike Hull**; Club Med; Commodore Cruise Line/Crown Cruise Line, **Jeff Stutin**; Costa Cruise Lines, **Linda Parrotta, Darren Oster**; Cruise West, **Maureen Camandona**; Crystal Cruises, **Mimi Weisband, Kristin Turner**; Cunard and Seabourn Cruise Line, **Bruce Good, Julie Davis**; Disney Cruise Line, **Jane Adams, Mark Jaronski**; First European/Festival Cruises; Holland America Line, **Erik Elvejord, Julianne Chase**; Lindblad Expeditions, **Amy Yankoviak**; Norwegian Cruise Line (Orient Lines, Norwegian Capricorn Line), **Fran Sevchik**; Princess Cruises and P & O Cruises, **Julie Benson, Denise Seomin**; Radisson Seven Seas Cruises; Regal Cruises; Residensea Ltd.; Renaissance Cruises, Royal Caribbean International, **Michelle Smith, Merle Jones**; Royal Olympic Cruises; St. Lawrence Cruise Lines; Sea Cloud Cruises; Silversea Cruises, **Dale Q. DiBello**; Star Clippers, **Alan Bell**; Star Cruises; Victoria Cruises; Windstar Cruises, **Mary Schimmelman, Sarah Johnson**; Cybercruises.com, Maritimematters.com.

PHOTO CREDIT: Cover-Star Clippers, Cover and interior-Carnival Cruise Line, Crystal Cruises, Holland America Line, Princess Cruises, Silversea Cruises, Star Clippers.

Cruise Chooser

Buyer's Guide to Cruises:
Bargains, Discounts & Deals
How to Get the Best for Less.

TABLE OF CONTENTS

VIP TIPS: How to Cruise as a VIP!

PART 4

Cruising Made Easy
A. **Money Well Spent**
B. **Service: Tip Guide**

E. **Destinations**
   Shore Excursions especially for you.
   Ports of Departure
   Cruising and the Environment.

PART 6

Postcards From the Past
A Brief Glance at Cruising's History.
Firsts

PART 7

Cruise Line Profiles
A. Cruise Line 'Personality'
B. Fleet
C. Passenger Type
D. Destinations
E. Programs
F. Highlights
G. New Ships
H. Special Deals
   plus NEW Web sites

PART 8

Cruise Chooser CYBERGUIDE
Easy list of *Money-Saving Web Sites*

PART 9

Cruise Chooser RESOURCE GUIDE

Books, Newsletters, Magazines & videos at your fingertips!

PART 10

Cruise Guides:

Cruise Guide for Active Adults
Cruise Guide for Children
Cruise Guide Credit Card Acceptance
Cruise Guide for Honeymooners
Cruise Guide for On-Board Meeting Facilities
Cruise Guide for Lean and Light Shipboard Cuisine
Cruise Guide for On-Board Spa Facilities
Cruise Guide for Worldwide Destinations
(Source: Cruise Lines International Association, CLIA)

INDEX

PART 1

Just Imagine Yourself on a Cruise!

- ◆ Why Cruise?
- ◆ Top 40 Questions
- ◆ Who Cruises?
- ◆ Personality Quiz
  Avoid Cruise Pitfall #1
  Take this quiz.

Why Cruise?

What makes cruises so popular? What's in it for me? What does a cruise have to offer me?

Now you know a cruise is a great vacation value - but there's much more to cruising than getting a great deal. Whether you're a savvy old salt or a first time cruiser you'll appreciate what makes cruises so popular: cuisine, service, entertainment, value added programs.

The **F**ood!

Eight meals a day is just the beginning! You'll enjoy bountiful midnight buffets, gourmet dining, Pizza parlors and Italian or Japanese restaurants. Whether you're having breakfast in bed, lunch on the Lido deck or dining with the captain - you can relax - everything's included in the price of your cruise. Cruising is so convenient - you can cruise to exotic foreign lands without the hassles of finding restaurants, reading menus and figuring out the exchange rate.

Cruise cuisine varies from simple American-style fare to five-course fine dining. Each day brings new delicious variety: soups, appetizers, lobster or Angus beef; freshly-made rolls and bread and mouth-watering desserts. It's easy to request light, lean, low sodium or vegetarian meals. You'll feel at home when your waiter remembers you like your steak medium-rare.

It's impossible to go hungry- in addition to breakfast, lunch and dinner you'll want to try the afternoon tea, 24-hour room service, hot and cold appetizers at happy hour and themed nightly buffets complete with hand-carved fruit and ice sculptures.

Drinks

On most ships, beverages other than coffee, tea, lemonade and some juices must be purchased separately. Sodas and alcoholic beverages may be paid for with cash, credit card or billed to your onboard credit account. A few deluxe lines do include all beverages in their fares.

Your Ship

All aboard for the vacation of your dreams! Shopping, dining, relaxing? Of course! Rock climbing and ice skating? You've got it! Your ship offers you all the amenities and activities of a fine resort plus travel to exciting ports. Whatever you like to do, however you'd like to spend your vacation; from polishing your golf game, to practicing your figure-eights, there's a ship for you.

Service!

"Let us pamper you," say the genuine smiles of your cruise staff. Personal service and attention is the rule from the time you come aboard. You'll feel like a VIP as you have your photo taken by the ship's photographer

and are greeted by white-gloved room stewards. You'll be shown to your stateroom as your luggage is brought up from the terminal. Meet your stateroom steward; he or she can be counted on for attentive service and thorough daily housekeeping.

Questions? Concerns? The knowledgeable purser and his staff are always available with answers and assistance. Your galley and dining room staff work hard to provide varied menus and excellent service. Mirrors gleam, brass shines and used glassware disappears as the smallest details are attended to by a busy janitorial staff. You'll sense the proud stewardship of carpenters and painters as they keep their vessel ship-shape.

Don't be shy to talk with the entertainers and cruise staff. They're chosen not only for their creative talents but their friendly spirit as well. Ladies need never feel like wallflowers with Gentleman Hosts aboard and children are well looked after by an energetic team of youth counselors. At the end of another exciting day; return to your comfortable stateroom, your bed freshly made with chocolates on the pillow.

Romance!

Live your fantasy - cruises are made for romance! Now it's your turn. Rekindle the thrill of when the two of you first met. Celebrate your private victories. Enjoy some free time together.
Meet that special someone and let the sparks fly. Start something!

Steal away with your sweetheart and a bottle of bubbly for a steamy dip in the Jacuzzi. Tell secrets under starlit skies. Stroll hand-in-hand along sugar-sand beaches where the only footprints you see are your own. Explore your world - just the two of you.

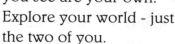

Fun! Fun! Fun!

Whatever floats your boat - there's plenty of fun for everyone. What's your vacation fantasy? Cruising

offers elaborate Broadway-style musicals, cabaret revues, magic, comedy, intimate piano bars and dancing under the stars. You can meet internationally-acclaimed entertainers, guest lecturers and sports legends onboard.

Venture ashore to learn about native culture or get up-close to rare wildlife. Win big with Vegas-caliber casino action and go shopping in an exotic bazaar.

The People

You'll feel at home while you meet people from around the world. It's easy to find that small-town

camaraderie on a cruise, where stress slips away and spirits rise. Bring your address book to add names of new-found friends. A cruise offers the perfect atmosphere for new or renewed friendships.

The Spa!

Because you're worth it, reserve your massage or beauty treatment right away. Enjoy being pampered by professionals in a state-of-the-art spa. Head to toe - you'll find the latest in health and beauty aboard ship.

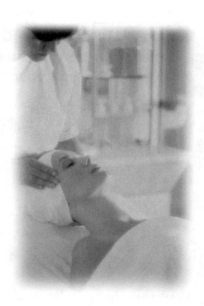

VIP Style

Your friends will envy you! The stories you'll have to tell...and you'll have photos to prove it. If your friends could see you now; dressed to kill at the cap-

tain's cocktail party and laughing with new-found friends after dinner at the captain's table. Wait 'till they hear about your adventures ashore in exotic ports; your win in the casino, luxurious massages, and breakfasts in bed. You are the VIP of this vacation. (Of course, you can invite your friends to join you next time.)

Fascinating **P**orts

Travel in style - safely and comfortably - to just about anywhere you've dreamed of. Visit the world's finest ports and join in memorable shore excursions. Snorkeling? Bicycling? Parasailing? Why not?!

Happy **Kids!**

Will the children enjoy cruising? You bet! More ships than ever before offer children's services: year-round supervised activities, entertainment for separate age groups and baby-sitting. Cruising is a fun family vacation. See *The Perfect Cruise for You: Traveling with Children.*

Expert Answers to the Top 40 Questions on Cruise Vacations

1. Is cruising affordable and a good vacation value?

Easy and Convenient: Cruising is convenient - you can relax and enjoy yourself without the hassles involved in pleasing everyone. You unpack once - no hauling luggage around. Dining is easy, saving you the effort of finding a restaurant, parking space, reading a foreign menu or paying with foreign currency.

Care-free: Your floating resort travels with you to the best vacation places and you don't need to lift a finger. Isn't it about time someone waited on you?! The friendly cruise staff provides personal service that's hard to find ashore.

Good Value: Cruising is an affordable and value-packed vacation. It's basic math - see the cruise Vs land-based vacation comparison chart. Your cruise includes all meals, entertainment and accommodations - some cruise lines even include tips and all beverages in the package price.

Fun: Cruising offers a variety of dining, entertainment and travel experiences. There's plenty to choose from; plenty to please everyone. The whole family will enjoy a fun, secure and care-free vacation.

See *The Best for Less: Bargains, Discounts & Deals.*

Cost Comparison Worksheet:
Typical Air/Sea Cruise Vacation vs Typical Land-based Vacation.

Cruise		Land
Cruise Fare	$	N/A
Room	Included	$
Transportation (port to port)	Included	$
Ground Transfers	Included	$
Breakfast	Included	$
Lunch	Included	$
Dinner	Included	$
Midnight Buffet	Included	$
Sports Activities	Included	$
Parties	Included	$
Entertainment	Included	$
Disco	Included	$
Nightclub Shows	Included	$
Airfare	Included	$
TOTAL	$	$

Source:2000 Cruise Market Profile Study, Cruise Lines International Association, CLIA.

2. How long are cruises?

You choose how much of your vacation time to spend on a cruise. Take a two night weekend getaway or a 3- or 4-night cruise. Seven-night voyages are still the most popular; although many seasoned sailors love 10- and 12-night trips or around-the-world adventures. There's a cruise to fit your schedule and help you make the most of your vacation time.

3. Where can I go? *Where do you want to go?*

You name it - there's a cruise to take you there. It's the fun and easy way to visit an exotic location for the first time or return to a old favorite. See the *Cruise Destination Guide* and start packing for your dream vacation!

4. Will I get to do what I want to do?

You can do it all or nothing at all. Join in scheduled activities, shows and shore excursions or make your own way. You're in charge - free to relax and enjoy your vacation. See *The Perfect Cruise for You.*

5. Will I be comfortable, safe and secure?

Your personal enjoyment, safety and security is the cruise line's main priority! All cruise ships are subject to strict international standards and regulations set forth by the International Maritime Organization (IMO). The US Coast Guard holds quarterly inspections of ships calling at US ports, and the cruise industry is also regulated by 8 other US government agencies. See more details on security measures in *Cruising Made Easy.*

6. Will I be entertained?

7. Will it be fun?

8. What's there to do?

9. Do I have to participate in the activities?

10. Will I get bored?

11. Will I feel confined?

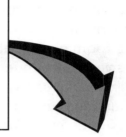

It's your cruise, your custom vacation. Do it all or nothing at all! Do what you want to do! Spend your days and nights exactly as you like. The rules really are different out there. Cruises are truly versatile - offering visits to exciting ports of call with shore excursions, sightseeing and shopping. You can shop to you drop, beach it, parasail, snorkel, SCUBA, sightsee and so much more.

On board your floating resort you can work on your tan or your golf game, read a classic or the latest trash. Meet friends at the fitness center for dance/aerobics/yoga class. Get in a workout on the virtual reality exercise bikes or weight-training equipment. Pamper yourself with a rejuvenating massage and aromatherapy, have your hair styled or your nails manicured, tour the bridge or the galley, take in a port lecture or a workshop on the stock market, gourmet cooking or gaming strategy.

Relax! Lounge in your comfortable stateroom with the TV or a video or escape with a novel to your favorite deck chair. Make yourself at home - as you travel the world. See the *Cruise Activities Guide.*

12. What's there to do at night?

Join friends at your favorite meeting place for conversation or a drink before dinner. Enjoy VIP treatment and delicious food at a well-staffed dining room or specialty restaurant. Stroll with your sweetheart under the stars, or join the fun in the disco. Choose from the latest Broadway-style entertainment in state-of -the-art showrooms; magic; comedy or Caribbean steel drums poolside.

Head to the casino for another round of black jack or roulette. How will you spend your winnings? A new swimsuit? Sparkling jewelry? Souvenirs for friends back home? There's still time to catch a first-run movie and don't forget the midnight buffet!

13. How do I get the most for my money?

Get Cruise Chooser - and get the best vacation values, bargains, discounts and deals. With countless insider's tips and more than 25 popular discount programs it's easy for us to offer our Cruise Chooser $500 Guarantee. We guarantee you'll save at least $500 on your next cruise - or get your money back. Cruise Chooser will refund the price of your book.

Use Cruise Chooser and you're sure to get the best for less!

14. How do I book a cruise?

Shop online and see a qualified travel agent, preferably a cruise specialist. See *The Best for Less, Cruise Chooser Cyberguide*.

14

15. Are all ships and cruises fairly similar?

There's a voyage and a vessel just for you. Just like different cars - each ship has her own personality. Some folks prefer a Mustang convertible; others a Mercedes, Cadillac, Mini-van or Sport Utility Vehicle. There's a cruise that fits your lifestyle. You'll feel at home and at ease. Cruise lines are working overtime to establish not only a brand identity for their fleet but individual 'personalities' for each ship. See *Cruise Line Profiles.*

16. What's an air/sea cruise?

Some cruise lines offer packages including the cruise and air transportation to and from the port. Their special arrangements with air lines, or airline partnership/ownership means lower rates for you. Check the brochures and advertisements for cruise-only and cruise plus air rates. Consult with your travel agent to get the best air travel rates. See *The Best for Less: Bargains, Discounts & Deals.*

17. Can I book on short notice?

Last minute or "Pier-head jump" sales can save you money - but your choice of accommodations and sailing dates will be limited. A better bet is an 'advance' or 'early booking discount', which gives you a broader choice of staterooms and departure dates. For 25 popular discounts see *The Best for Less.*

18. Do I need a passport? Which documents do I need in order to cruise? Where do I get them? How long will it take to receive them?

Ask your travel agent, read the cruise line brochure carefully and see *Cruising Made Easy* for specific step-by-step directions on how to get the correct documents.

19. Are there different classes of service?

Cruise line travelers no longer adhere to a social caste system of First, Second and Steerage Class. Service aboard your floating resort varies according to the staff to passenger ratio, nationality of staff, size and style of ship and cruise line 'personality.' Award-winning service is listed in the *Best of the Best Awards* at our Web site **www.cruisechooser.com**.

20. What's there to do in port?

Cruise ships call at a variety of destinations offering shore excursions, sightseeing and shopping. You can shop to you drop, beach it, parasail, snorkel, SCUBA, sightsee and more. Be welcomed 'home' to villages of native islanders, enjoy a private showing of folklore dance and drama, explore ancient ruins, ride a bicycle into a volcano, cross rope bridges through the rainforest, pan for gold and so much more. See *The Perfect Cruise for You.*

21. Do cruise lines welcome families with kids?

Do they ever! Many cruise lines offer comprehensive children's programs with full-time professional youth counselors, kid's play and game rooms, children's swimming pools, children's shore excursions, baby sitting, special menu's and even their own daily program delivered to your door. For examples of children's programs see the *Cruise Guide for Children.*

22. Is there a charge for entertainment?

Most of the shipboard entertainment is included in the price of your cruise vacation: Broadway-style or Vegas-style shows, magic, comedy, quartets and duos, vocalists, contests, a piano bar, poolside steel-drum bands. You can hit the disco or dance under the stars, or try your luck in the casino. Save time for the fitness center, where you'll find dance/aerobics/yoga classes; virtual reality exercise bikes or weight-training equipment.

For the price of your ticket you'll also enjoy ship tours of the bridge or galley, workshops and port lectures. Special theme cruises feature wine-tastings and special appearances by celebrities. First-run movies and computer labs are also available on many ships.

23. Is it easy to meet people? Will there be people like me?

Ask anyone who has cruised and although they may not remember the name of their last ship, they'll never forget the good friends they've made on vacation. That's what sets cruising apart from typical land-based vacations, getaways and family trips. You can revel in the privacy of your own verandah or be right in the middle of things with old and new friends. Take the *Cruise Chooser Personality Quiz*.

24. & 25. What to pack? • Whatever shall I wear?

Night comes and it's time to dress to the nines or relax at the poolside bar . Aboard most ships, the fashion tends toward casual with a few dressy evenings or one formal night. All cruise lines suggest clothing guidelines in their brochures, videos and Web sites. Talk with your travel agent for first-hand advice on what to wear. There's a cruise to suit your vacation lifestyle and wardrobe. See the **clothing checklists** in *Cruising Made Easy*.

26. Can I use my appliances: hair dryer, shaver, laptop, cell phone, Gameboy?

Bring all you want. Most ships offer dual voltage or converters for differing types of appliances. Some cruise lines supply hair dryers in your stateroom. Consult your travel agent.

27. Can singles have fun on a cruise?

Yes! Cruising is popular with singles because it offers camaraderie, safety and convenience. See *Cruise Guide for Singles, The Perfect Cruise for You*.

28. Can we celebrate a "special" day?

Yes! Whether it's your birthday, honeymoon, anniversary or renewal of vows you are celebrating, your travel agent and cruise staff can arrange for services and amenities to make your event memorable. See *Cruising Made Easy*.

29. Are religious holidays celebrated onboard?

Many cruise ships provide a interdenominational chapel and several lines sail with a priest or minister aboard, adding a rabbi during Jewish holidays.

30. Is cruising right for wedding parties? Or honeymooners?

Cruises are made for romance and new beginnings. See *Cruise Guide for Honeymooners*.

31. Can we stay in touch with friends, family and business back home?

Not to worry, staying in touch has become even easier, with many ships offering onboard computer e-mail access. Its easy to call from aboard ship or in port and postcards sent from afar will remain treasured souvenirs forever.

32. What about tipping?

Tipping is easy with the *Tip Guide* found in *Cruising Made Easy*.

33. Are there medical services onboard?

Your ship's physician and nursing staff is on-call 24-hours and offers convenient office hours. Emergency care is their specialty. See *Cruising Made Easy*.

34. Are there laundry services aboard?

All ships can handle your laundry and dry cleaning needs. You'll also find 24-hour passenger laundries.

35. Do cruise lines accept group bookings?

Yes! For group discounts and planning tips see *The Best for Less*. More groups and associations are discovering that a cruise offers the best value in an all-inclusive, easy-to-plan get-together. Chances are some of your fellow cruisers will be traveling with their family reunions, school reunion, graduation class, club or church convention.

36. Are there meeting rooms onboard?

Your travel agent can recommend the best shipboard facilities for your meeting or celebration. The cruise lines cater to groups of 50 to 500 or more. The business world is taking advantage of high-tech facilities aboard newer ships, which can easily accommodate business and corporate meetings, seminars, conferences, conventions and trade shows.

Meeting planners rejoice! Most cruise lines have special group and incentive sales departments. Several of the newest ships offer complete audio and video technology, and you'll even find complete television broadcast services at sea. See *Trends in Cruising*.

37. Can I extend my cruise vacation?

Make the most of your vacation with a pre-or post-cruise stay-over at the port of departure city. See *The Best for Less*.

38. Will I get sea sick?

Today's ships have come a long way in eliminating motion-sickness. New propulsion technology and hull designs make cruising as comfortable as being ashore. For suggestions on traveling in good health see *Cruising Made Easy*.

39. What does a ship's registry or 'flag' mean?

The Liberian (Bahamian, British, Greek, Netherlands, Norwegian or Panamanian) flag signifies the ship's country of registration. Ocean-going vessels engaged in international commerce, including passenger cruise ships, must be registered in order to operate in international waters. US law prohibits any ship not built in the US from flying a US flag. 80 percent of the vessels calling on the US are non-US flag vessels.

40. What's the $500 question?

For years, fat cat insiders have lived high on the hog, they travel in style and never, never pay retail. Here's your chance to get even! Cruise Chooser will show you how to shop like a seasoned sailor.

Use the money-saving tips in Cruise Chooser and save $500 on your next cruise vacation, Guaranteed!

We're so confident that Cruise Chooser will save you big money on your next cruise - we've put it in writing. (See *$500 Guarantee* in the *Foreward*)

Get Cruise Chooser and get the Best for Less!

WHO CRUISES: Where Do You Fit In?

You're bound to feel comfortable and at ease traveling with your fellow cruisers. Here's a profile of the types of travelers who cruise. Perhaps you'll recognize yourself or a friend!

Who is Cruising: By the Numbers

Who cruises? Cruising is no longer for the 'blue-haired and bejeweled,' it's an all-ages vacation value! You'll find single men and women, couples of all ages, friends and families. Enjoy the journey with travelers celebrating honeymoons, anniversaries and family reunions. You'll meet people from across the nation and around the world. Your fellow travelers will likely be a member of the burgeoning boomer generation.

Behold the Baby Boomers!

36% of all US travelers and 29% of the world's overall population are Baby Boomers, according to Travel Industry Association figures and US Census estimates. The Cruise Lines International Association, CLIA, studies show 53% of the cruising public are "baby boomers" ages 45-54, and these vacationers want it all! They usually travel several weeks a year, taking a 7-10 day vacation plus two or more long weekends or getaways. Most boomers desire a vacation that includes flexibility, adventure, several dining options and choice of evening entertainment. They're open to 'newer', lesser-known destinations, and often their vacation focuses on fun, adventure or a sports activity.

CLIA, assigns recent cruising Baby Boomers to six market segments: Restless Baby Boomers, Enthusiastic Baby Boomers, Luxury Seekers, Consummate Shoppers, Explorers and Ship Buffs.

Restless Baby Boomers (33%) are new to cruising. They would like to cruise again; are cost conscious; and are trying different, affordable vacations. 59% of these young and restless travelers are first-time cruisers.

Enthusiastic Baby Boomers (20%) are excited about cruising and its many activities. They live intense, stressful lives and look for escape and relaxation in vacations. They're looking to "get away from it all."

Luxury Seekers (14%) can afford a deluxe vacation and are willing to spend money for deluxe accommodations and pampering. These travelers have high expectations and are well-traveled.

Consummate Shoppers (16%) are looking for the best value (not necessarily the cheapest) in a cruise vacation. They are committed cruisers and choose to cruise over other vacations.

Explorers (11%) are well-educated, well-traveled individuals with an intellectual interest and curiosity about different destinations. They are seeking alternative destinations and new experiences.

Ship Buffs (6%) are usually the most senior segment. They have cruised extensively and demand in-depth itineraries with comfortable surroundings.

Baby Boomers, Age 45-54 Control More Than 50 Percent of US Wealth:

$7 trillion of the nation's assets.

Baby boomers are likely to be well-traveled and view travel as a right, not a luxury. A generation raised on Jane Fonda workouts and Richard Simmons' diets, these travelers are in better shape than previous generations and seek out more active vacations.

By the year 2000, 28% of the US population, or about 74 million people will be in their 50's.

Every 7 1/2 seconds someone turns 50 -- approximately 7,000 people every day.

In 2020, 37% or more than 110 million people in the US will be over 50.

Younger, Mature Travelers

Ages 55-70, these travelers are interested in intellectual and spiritual stimulation. They enjoy discovering new places, and love setting their own course. They also like the structure of escorted tours and cruises. These travelers are attracted to itineraries featuring cultural and historical destinations.

Multigenerational Travelers

'Multigenerational' groups or families with children are the fastest growing cruise population. Parents, single-parents, grandparents and children come together on a cruise. It's not unusual to find three to four generations of a family reunited on a Caribbean voyage. Every member of the family can look forward to a fun, safe, educational and hassle-free vacation.

Gen X

The generation x'ers, ages 18-35, juggle work, school, church and community activities at a frenetic pace. These dual-income couples or families want more out of a vacation and they're willing to pay for it. With ample funds but limited vacation time, Gen X'rs prefer active 'accomplishment vacations,' such as mountain climbing or bicycle riding over 'lazy retreats' in prestigious resorts. These cruisers are in search of active, achievement-oriented vacations which offer an 'antidote' to civilization and their hectic lives.

Lifestyles of the Well-Traveled

How much does your lifestyle influence your choice of vacation? Can you predict who your fellow cruisers will be based on demographics, psycho-graphics and broad economic trends? Your lifestyle, age, economic status and 'generational outlook,' or attitude on travel all have a dramatic impact on vacation choices, say authors and travel industry consultants, Gary Langer and Lynne Sorensen, CTC.

Here's how demographic trends help people choose their cruise:

1. *More families onboard:* Americans are having fewer children, later in life; and traveling with them more. Today's families view travel more as a 'given right' than a privileged luxury.

'Multi-generational' groups or families with children are part of the fastest growing segment of the cruising population. Parents, single-parents, grandparents and children or three generations of family; kids and adults find there's something for everyone on a cruise.

2. *More Baby Boomers 45-54 and mature travelers 55-70 choose to cruise:* They're healthier, wealthier and ready to spend that disposable cash on a cruise vacation.

3. *More single sailors:* Cruises attract fun-seeking singles of all ages. Single women travelers (single, widowed, divorced) appreciate the personal service, security and companionship a cruise offers. It's easy and convenient, since your travel to and from the cruise ship and baggage handling are taken care of. (Pack all you want!)

It's easy to meet other singles aboard and Sign up for a shore excursion and sightsee safely - cruising gives you the 'built in' advantage of 'safety-in-numbers.'

Do these profiles remind you of anyone?
Yourself perhaps? Your spouse, friends or family? We expect you'll feel comfortable and at ease traveling with your fellow cruisers. You might even meet that 'special someone' or fall in love all over again!

Now that you know more about your fellow passengers, **get to know your own vacation personality profile & avoid Cruise Pitfall #1:** Cruise Mismatch-buying a cruise simply because it is on sale, without knowing if it fits *your* cruise vacation personality. **Take this quiz and find the perfect fit!** ➡

Cruise Personality Quiz

1. What did you do on your last vacation?
   1) Resort Vacation, Spa, Beaches
   2) City and Countryside Touring
   3) Theme Park, Casino
   4) Cycling, Hiking, Scuba diving

2. Which of the following vacation experiences
have you had in the past 3 years?
   1) Resort, Spa, Beach Resort
   2) European Capital Cities, Ancient Ruins
   3) Las Vegas, Theme park, Sports Vacation
      (golf, tennis, diving)
   4) Safari, Camping, Eco-adventure

3. On Vacation, which places interest you most?
   1) beaches as far as the eye can see
   2) country roads & ancient villages
   3) big city lights
   4) wilderness

4. What have you always wanted to do if you
   had the chance?
   1) spend a day at the spa for 'the works.'
   2) have your photo taken at the pyramids
   3) Win Big at the newest casinos
   4) go rafting on wild river rapids

5. How do you prefer to dress while on vacation?
    1) swimsuit and suntan lotion
    2) blue jeans and binoculars
    3) glamorous gowns and tuxedo or black tie
    4) hiking boots and snow skis

6. What sort of lifestyle or activities do you enjoy on weekends?
    1) shopping, dining, lounging by the pool
    2) antiquing, reading, attending lectures
    3) golfing, attending sporting events
    4) bicycle races and marathons

7. What activities have you always wanted to try?
    1) shower in a waterfall, go bare on the beach
    2) Meet giraffes or polar bear-on their turf
    3) see a Broadway show - in the front row
    4) cross the rainforest by rope bridges

8. Where have you always wanted to visit?
    1) Hawaiian Islands
    2) Rome
    3) Monte Carlo
    4) Tahiti

9. What is your favorite Dining experience?
    1) breakfast in bed
    2) Caribbean or French cuisine
    3) Top Angus steak cooked to order
    4) Native Jamaican or Middle-Eastern delicacies

10. Which activity is your kind of Fun ?

1) Enjoy a relaxing aromatherapy session or seaweed bath.
2) See India's Taj Mahal.
3) Ride a helicopter over a waterfall.
4) Ride horseback through jungles.

Add your answers by the number

Example:

Answer 1) equals 1 point, Answer 2) equals 2 points, etc.

Match your total number of points:

Hedonist: 8-15 points

Explorer: 16-23 points

Action Seeker: 24-31 points

Adventurer: 32 + points

Hedonist

You who are a Hedonist live life to its fullest. Pleasure is your principal aim. Gourmet living appeals to you, so let your stateroom steward and waiter know of your special requests. Be pampered: Make your Spa reservations upon arrival Relax and savor the moment: stake out your favorite deck chair poolside or join your many friends for shoreside shopping or onboard pleasures of Broadway-style entertainment. Your next vacation will deliver a world full of pleasure

Explorer

You who are an Explorer relish the discovery of authentic culture, art and dining. You are open to journey off the beaten path in order to experience the pulse of a destination. Your enthusiasm and energy make you the perfect organizer of groups, though you never hesitate to venture out on your own. Your next vacation will open to a world of exciting experiences.

Action Seeker

Action Seeker, you're likely to be the center of attention at home in the casino or the dance floor. Your day is non-stop, with just enough time for a quick costume change. You do everything first-class and will want extra storage in stateroom for an extensive wardrobe and for new purchases. Your next vacation will provide a whirlwind of activity.

Adventurer

Adventurer, cruising has adapted to meet your high-octane approach to life. Mornings may find you snorkeling Grand Cayman, while afternoons you're hiking in a tropical rainforest. The rock-climbing walls and ice-skating rinks were added with you in mind. Nights find you winning at the casino and dancing under the stars. Ask your travel agent to reserve your shore excursions in advance. Your next vacation promises unforgettable adventure.

Visit **www.cruisechooser.com** to match your Cruise Personality with the right cruise at the best price!

PART 2
How to Choose the Right Cruise for You!

A. **Cruises to Fit Your Lifestyle**
- Solo Traveler
- Babyboomers
- Grandparents & Grandchildren
- Mature Traveler
- Families with Children
- Disabled Traveler
- Gay and Lesbian Traveler
- Wedding Parties and Honeymooners

Includes: Cruise Chooser Checklists

B. **The Perfect Stateroom**

Plus: How to Avoid Cruise Choosing Pitfall # 2

Cruise Choosing Pitfall #2
AS SEEN ON TV

Ipso facto "By the fact itself; by the mere fact." Buying a cruise solely because you like the TV commercial. Those cruise line advertisements are irresistible. Dancing starfish beckon you to sail away today, and who doesn't dream of being served tropical drinks - while you float lazily on a raft?!

How can you be sure this cruise will meet *your* vacation needs and expectations?

First, see how cruise lines cater to all types of travelers in *Cruises to Fit your Lifestyle.* Next, see which cruise lines and ships score highest in the *Cruise Chooser Best of the Best Awards,* found at our Web site **www.cruisechooser.com**.

A. Cruises to Fit Your Lifestyle.

Another reason cruises are becoming more popular is that a cruise vacation easily accommodates many types of travelers. Whether you travel as a couple, solo, with children or with a group - there's a perfect cruise just for you.

- Solo Traveler
- Babyboomers
- Mature Traveler
- Families with Children
- Grandparents & Grandchildren
- Disabled Traveler
- Gay & Lesbian Traveler
- Wedding Parties & Honeymooners

SOLO TRAVELERS
   -- Savings programs
   --Gentleman Hosts
   --Resources: Travel Associations, Books, Web sites.

"A good traveling companion is easier to lose than find."

Must single travelers pay double the price?
   Almost all cruise fares are quoted as 'per person/double occupancy', meaning the fare covers one person's passage and assumes that a second fare-paying person is traveling with them and sharing their stateroom. Solo cruisers can be hit with a surcharge from 125 to 200 percent of the per person double occupancy rate.

Go solo and save 2 ways:
   "guaranteed share" fares allow you to pay the per-person double occupancy rate while the cruise line

attempts to match you with an appropriate solo roommate (same sex, age range, smoker/non smoker). If the sailing is not fully booked, you may keep your stateroom to yourself, at no extra charge.

"single occupancy" staterooms can still be found on older, classic ships - ask your travel agent about staterooms on such classics as NCL's Norway, Cunard's QE2, and American Hawaii's Independence.

example:

American Hawaii Cruises

Single Supplement Charge Category AAA through A add 100%; category B through G add 60%. Subject to availablity at time of booking. No single supplement charge for single cabins.

"I was a bit hesitant to travel alone - Eddie and I went everywhere together, for so many years," says Sue Ann.

"But at this stage of my life, there are so many places I want to see. My son is concerned for my safety. My daughter insists that I should take advantage of my good health and take all the trips I want. Can a single woman enjoy herself and stay safe while traveling alone?

Sue Ann's questions about solo travel echo the concerns of many widowed, divorced and single mature travelers - both women and men. Cruising makes it easy to travel on your own. Your transportation from airport to cruise terminal plus all your baggage handling is taken care of. It's easy to meet people aboard ship. Conversation and camaraderie come without effort. Sign up for a shore excursion where you'll travel safely as part of a group. A cruise is an effortless way to sample destinations for a future vacation.

ISO sophisticated traveler, who enjoys shopping, sightseeing, fine dining and fun! Ready to travel?!

Looking for a travel companion? Use your results from the *Cruise Chooser Personality Quiz* and ask your potential travel partner to take the quiz.

Love to Dance?!

Wallflowers are nowhere to be found on ships offering the popular Gentleman Host program, thanks to the gallant efforts of the late Richard Revnes. Revnes introduced an elite group of dancing and dining companions aboard Royal Cruise Line voyages. Their mission? No solo woman passenger would miss out on activities. The program proved so successful that it is now offered by more than half a dozen cruise lines. See *Cruise Guide for Singles.*

Resources: Travel clubs for single travelers

Going Solo Travel Club
187 Midlawn Close, S.E., Calgary, AB, T2XIA7, Canada, (888) 4-GO-SOLO. For singles of all ages.

Grand Circle Travel Club
Grand Circle Travel, Inc., 347 Congress St., Boston, MA 12210 617-350-7500, (800)248-3737

Join Grand Circle and add your name to a list of available travel companions; also receive their quarterly magazine with travel companion "want ads."

Merry Widows Tours
800-374 2689 You don't have to be widow to join other solo women travelers- singles and divorcées are welcome.

Partners-in-Travel
P.O. Box 491145, Los Angeles, CA 90049
(310) 476-4869.

Join Partners-in-Travel and receive a one-year subscription to their bi-monthly publication listing travelers in search of companions. Call to request free information on traveling solo.

Travel Companion Exchange
   P.O. Box 833, Amityville, NY 11701 (516) 454-0880,
   (800) 392-1256.
   Add your name and specifications to the
Exchange's travel companion list.

The Only Way to Travel
   7467 East Main Street, #3, Reynoldsburg, OH
   43068, [http://www.onlywaytotravel.com]
   Specializes in booking singles cruises.

Resources: Books
*Cruising Solo : The Single Traveler's Guide to
Adventure on the High Seas,* Maisel, Sally J., 1993,
Marin Publications; ISBN: 0934377146

Single's Guide to Cruise Vacations, Simenauer,
Jacqueline and Margaret Russell, 1997, Prima Pub;
ISBN: 0761503242

MATURE TRAVELER

   Congratulations! Chances are you've achieved
some freedom and a certain amount of disposable
income; you LOVE to travel and hate to pay full
price. Whether you're traveling solo, as a couple,
with friends or with your grandkids; the cruise lines
want your business and offer a variety of discounts
and savings just for mature travelers. See *The Best for
Less.*
   Carnival Cruise Lines expects to carry a record
500,000 guests over the age of 55 this year -- a full 30
percent of its overall passenger base.

Resources: travel clubs

Go Ahead Vacations,
   1 Memorial Drive, Cambridge, MA 02142
   (800)242-4686, (617) 252 6262 Worldwide cruises
   and other travel for those 55 and up.

Golden Age Travelers
   Pier 27, The Embarcadero, San Francisco, CA
   94111 (800)258-8800
   Subscribe to their quarterly newsletter for trips
   and discounts for travelers "50 and up."

Golden Companions
   Box 754, Pullman, WA 99163 (208) 858-2183
   Travel discounts, network of more than 1000
   travelers age 46 and older.

Partners for Travel
   Box 560337, Miami, FL 33256 (800) 866-5565
   Subscribe to their 'Over 50' travel club newsletter.
   Benefits include get-togethers and discounts.

Tips for the Senior Mature Traveler

1. Easy does it - moderation is key in diet - don't feel you have to eat, drink and do it all in one day. Take it easy sightseeing - many travelers use port calls to sample destinations, then return later for a more in-depth visit.

2. Your ship: Your travel agent is your best ally in finding a ship that supports your physical abilities. Speak candidly with your agent about any limitations - consider the ship's size, number of passengers, accessibility and whether it tenders or docks at ports.

3. Your stateroom: Work with your agent to get a stateroom located near elevators, 'amidships' (mid-way between bow and stern); close to public areas.

4. Medical facilities and care: See *Cruising Made Easy: Health, Safety & Security Tips.*

TRAVELING WITH CHILDREN

- *Cruise Chooser Checklists*
    Packing for your Children
    Safety for your Children
    Babies on Board
- *Helpful Charts*
    Baby-sitting Services
    CLIA Cruise Guide for Children
- *Preparing Children for a Cruise*
- *Sample Highlights of Children's Programs*
- *Pregnancy and cruising*
- *Resources: Books, Videos, Web sites*

Cruises Keep the Whole Family Entertained.

Which vacation will please everyone, from grandparents to grandchildren? At the top of your vacation shopping list should be the growing number of cruise lines catering to families. Families are the fastest-growing segment of the cruise business and cruise executives are already banking on young cruisers for future business.

Savvy cruise line executives have two goals in mind: to provide junior cruisers with the first of many unforgettable cruise vacations and secondly, to insure that youthful exuberance doesn't disrupt the vacations of fellow passengers.

> In 2001, Carnival Cruise Lines expects to carry a record 250,000 children aboard its ships

Junior cruisers are welcomed aboard with special children's menus, age-oriented shore excursions and their own daily activity schedule. Most ships offer supervised children's programming during the summer and on holiday sailings. Several cruise lines have beefed up their youth counselor staffs to offer year-round, fleet-wide youth counselors and baby-sitting services. Parents and grandparents can enjoy an activity on their own, knowing their children are also having fun in a safe environment.

The newest ships are built for families & fun. They feature year-round activities programs, expanded youth-counselor staffs and dedicated children's facilities. Look forward to more ships with family-size staterooms that sleep six; plus teen discos, kids-only pools, virtual-reality gamerooms and activity centers.

Hot Tip: Birds of a feather - cruise better together: Consider a cruise with programs for several age groups - your kids will have more fun with same-age playmates aboard. See *Cruise Guide for Children (end of book), Cruise Chooser's Best of the Best Awards,* at **www. cruisechooser.com**.

Extra Credit for Children (and Parents)

Take the kids cruising and you'll give them memorable experiences they'll never find in textbooks: new words in foreign languages, distant lands with exotic cultures and new friends from around the world. Bring an address book for names of new international pen-pals. Take home some foreign coins - for school reports and show-and-tell.

PREPARING CHILDREN FOR THE FAMILY CRUISE VACATION

When Lauri and Garry married, they promised each other that their honeymoon would be just the beginning of their travels together.

"Our twins Julie and Katie go everywhere with us - why not a cruise? We always ask our travel agent for an extra brochure for the girls. We keep it in the kitchen so the whole family can share," says Lauri.

"Our agent gave us a video about our Alaskan cruise," says Garry. "I've also found local video stores or the library carry videos on the Caribbean and Alaska. The girls are already talking about seeing grizzly bears!"

Resources: Video/ Web sites

Case of the Mystery Cruise: Mary-Kate & Ashley Olsen.

[http://www.vacationsonvideo.com/] Vacations on Video offers a comprehensive collection of vacation destinations. Since 1984, the world's largest distributor of cruise, tour and destination videos. (800) 841-6675.

[http://destinations.previewtravel.com/DestGuides/VideoWorld/] Preview Travel's easy to view footage of cruise regions and destinations.

Resources: books

The Caribbean Cruise Caper (The Hardy Boys Mystery Stories No 154), Dixon, Franklin W., Minstrel Books; ISBN: 067102549X

The Case of the Mystery Cruise (The Adventures of Mary Kate and Ashley, No 2) Thompson, Carol 1996

The Mystery Cruise (Boxcar Children, No 29), Warner, Gertrude Chandler, Albert Whitman & Co.

CHECKLIST: PACKING FOR YOUR CHILDREN

✔ Kids love souvenirs - so give them a vacation allowance before you leave port.

✔ Bring rolls of quarters for video games.

✔ Divide your children's clothes and gear between several suitcases - if one case is lost or left behind, you're OK.

✔ Toys: for the pool and beach - goggles, mask and snorkel, float, water wings, pool shoes.

✔ Toys: For the cruise terminal embarkation and down time: coloring books, crayons, markers, books, Walkman, Gameboy (and extra batteries), diary or travel log, pens, address book.

✔ "Nite Nite!" - Bring along a favorite toy or blanket and a night light for unfamiliar bathrooms.

✔ Pack plastic bags for wet swimsuits and dirty clothes.

CHECKLIST: SAFETY for YOUR CHILDREN

✔ Tour the ship together as soon as possible.

✔ Establish a 'Rendezvous Point' or meeting place for family members who become separated.

   If parents get lost they'll know to meet the kids at the gameroom or purser's desk.

✔ Show children where bathrooms are located and how to use the WC (Water Closet.)

✔ Introduce children to the pursers' staff and youth counselors.

CHECKLIST: BABIES ON BOARD

✔ Babies and toddlers are not invited aboard all cruise lines. Confirm minimum age limits.

✔ Baby-sitting services vary by cruise line and ship. Work closely with your travel agent and read the last pages of the cruise line brochure.

Sample Baby-Sitting Services

Carnival Cruise Lines: Baby-sitting services conducted by the youth staff in "Children's World" from 10 p.m. to 3 a.m., as well as from 8 a.m. to noon on port days for children under 2. The charge is $5 per hour for the first child and $3 for each additional child in the same family.

Holland America Line: Baby sitting is available on a staff volunteer basis.

NCL offers baby-sitting (individual or group) for a fee. Sitters are available between noon and 2 a.m.

Princess Cruises recently added in-port baby-sitting and extended day care hours past midnight on all ships. $4.00 per hour per child. It also lowered the minimum age to sail from 18 months to 12 months.

TIP

Pack extra
baby supplies:
diapers,
teething toys
and gel, pow-
ders and
creams, wipes.
While available
for purchase
aboard and in
port, prices
may be some-
what higher

than home. Some cruise lines provide
complimentary baby food or diapers.

Pregnancy on board

Standard cruise line regulations regarding preg-
nant passengers are as follows:

Pregnancy must be regarded as a medical condition. An expectant mother's application for passage
must be accompanied by a medical certificate estab-
lishing her due date and fitness to travel, and are
subject to the following conditions. The cruise line
will not be responsible or liable for any complica-
tions of pregnancy which arise or occur during the
cruise. The cruise line will not accept guests who will
have entered their 24th week of pregnancy by the
time their travel with the cruise line concludes.

"Hey Sam, Don't Forget your Basketball"

Janet is taking her grandchildren Daryl, Sam and Eleanor on an NCL Sports Illustrated Afloat™ cruise. This time there will be NBA basketball players signing autographs and teaching workshops. Sam's looking forward to working out the finer points of his lay up with the pros. Daryl plans to tour the bridge and meet the Captain, while Eleanor can't wait to snorkel in the Caribbean Sea. There's enough going on to keep everyone busy - so Jan can work on her tan!

HIGHLIGHTS OF OUTSTANDING CHILDREN'S FACILITIES & PROGRAMS

The following highlights will give you a sense of what cruises offer children; including special menus, activities, facilities and age-specific shore excursions. This is a partial listing of cruise lines and their children's programs. Consult your travel agent for pricing and details.

Carnival's famous pool slides make it hard to return home to a plain-old-pool. How many times can you go down the Triumph's 114-foot -long cascading water slide?

CARNIVAL CRUISE LINES

"Camp Carnival" features a wide variety of age-appropriate activities from 9 a.m. to 10 p.m., conducted by the lines' 100-member fleet-wide youth staff. Sample activities include puppet shows, sing-a-longs and face painting for the younger cruisers, while older kids enjoy talent shows, jewelry-making sessions, dance classes and scavenger hunts.

Teen-oriented activities include late-night movies, pool parties, Ping-Pong and video game tournaments and parties. The Carnival Paradise offers "Children's World," a 2,500-square-foot playroom overlooks the main pool area. There's fun for all ages with a computer lab, 16-monitor video wall, arts-and-crafts center, activity center with toys, puzzles, games and a climbing maze. The outdoor play area offers playground equipment such as jungle gyms and mini-basketball hoops, along with a schooner-shaped playhouse. Children of all ages flock to "Virtual World," a high-tech gaming and entertainment center with the latest in video and arcade games, including virtual reality games.

Parents will appreciate the complete children's menu at all meals, as well as a 24-hour pizzeria serving up seven different kinds of pizza and calzone. Complimentary self-serve ice cream and frozen yogurt are available and "Fountain Fun Cards" are on-sale; good for unlimited soft drinks.

DISNEY CRUISE LINE
Especially for Kids

With almost an entire deck devoted to age-specific children's programs, your kids will want to join the fun at Disney's Oceaneer Club or Disney's Oceaneer Lab. Wanna' dress up like the Little Mermaid? Play a part in a Bahamian legend? Dig for treasure on Castaway Cay, Disney's private island? There's enough fun for everyone from making a batch of "Flubber," to learning the sailor's craft of scrimshaw or playing a part in a 'Walt Disney Theatre production'.

Sample activities:

Ages 3-5: Do Si Do with Snow White, Flounder's Fish Tales interactive puppet show.

Ages 6-8: Animation Antics: Introduction to simple animation techniques, Pirate Story-teller.

Ages 9-10: Making TV commercials, Villainous Ventures Mysteries.

Ages 11-12: Marblemania: design the ultimate marble racetrack; Goofin' Around with Animation: create your own flipbook to take home!

Especially for Teens

Imagine a New York-style coffeehouse with music, games, large-screen TV, a lounge area, a coffee bar, and shipboard programs like photography, movie making, and improvisational acting. Teens will appreciate the teens-only areas of Disney's Castaway Cay, where they can snorkel, bike, and kayak with their friends.

Disney Cruise Line makes sure adults have fun too; both ships feature adults-only lounges, bars, films, entertainment. Adults will also enjoy their own gourmet restaurant and swiming pool.

HOLLAND AMERICA LINE

Holland America's Club HAL recognizes young cruisers from the first night of their cruise - with a special welcome aboard from the Club HAL director. Club HAL's daily program is slipped under your cabin door each night along with the ship's daily activity guide. Each sea day is planned with at least one age-appropriate activity in the morning, afternoon and evening. There's an activity for three age groups: ages 5-8, 'tweens' ages 9-12 and teens, ages 13-17.

Club HAL activities include games and sports contests, scavenger or autograph hunts, candy bar bingo, disco parties, movie nights, a pizza party, a "coketail" party, coloring contests and show-and-tell time. Youngsters who participate receive a Club HAL T-shirt.

Kids-Only!

Holland America Line now offers Kids-only shore excursions. On HAL's 'Float Plane Adventure,' teens get to see Alaska's marvelous wilderness through the eyes of an eagle! A flight aboard an authentic Alaska bush plane allows spectacular views of scenic boat harbors, snow capped peaks and waterfalls in and around Ketchikan, Deer Mountain and Tongass National Forest.

'Giant Totems' helps 6-12 year olds immerse themselves in the stories carved in 100-year-old totem poles; learn about Native Alaskan culture and try their hand at traditional crafts. (That'll give em something to report on in their next "What I did last summer" assignment...)

On Caribbean voyages, HAL offers kids-and teens-only shore excursion at private island Half Moon Cay. 'X' marks the spot for Kids 6-12 - young treasure hunters gear up as pirates and use a marked map with clues to find the mother lode. Teens can dance and swoon under the moon at the beach party with snacks, music, beach volleyball and games.

NORWEGIAN CRUISE LINE

Kids Crew® offers year-round youth coordinators for kids 6-12, and teen coordinators for teenagers 13-17. During the summer months, winter break, Easter, Thanksgiving, Christmas and New Year's, NCL has coordinators for children 3-5.

NCL offers baby-sitting (individual or group) for a fee. Sitters are available between noon and 2 a.m.

PRINCESS CRUISES
Love Boat Kids

On Sky, Sun, Dawn, Sea, Ocean and Grand Princess, you'll find complete Youth and Teen Centers with arts and crafts, board games, movies, discos and video games.

Sun, Dawn, Sea, Ocean and Grand Princess even offer a toddler's play area and theater, a dolls' house, a castle, computers and ice-cream kiosk. Aboard the Grand Princess, kids have their own deck space with a whale's tail slide and splash pool. Teens will enjoy their own Jacuzzi and sunning area.

Other children's programs include "Save Our Seas" which involves kids in activities and special shore excursions based on ecology and stewardship of the oceans.

Princess Cay, the line's private Bahamian island features Pelican's Perch, a supervised play area with a pirate ship playground and sandbox. Teens can swim and snorkel, ride a banana boat or play beach volleyball.

Junior passengers, AKA "mermaids" and "sailors," can now enjoy their favorite foods 24-hours-a-day. The special evening bistro menu just for children is offered as an alternative to the ship's formal dining room and other alternative dining venues. Kids will appreciate the Buccaneer Burger, High Seas Hot Dog, Spaghetti Snakes, Fish Sticks, Chick-Chick-Chicken Fingers, and even "PB & J" Sandwiches. Kid-friendly fare is also available at many of Princess' other dining areas, including the main dining room, pizzeria, poolside hamburger grill, and ice cream bar.

ROYAL CARIBBEAN INTERNATIONAL

Settle in with the whole family in special suites that sleep six. Royal Caribbean offers separate children's playrooms, a teens-only disco and special menus suited to a kid's taste. Children and teens receive "Compass" itineraries, highlighting the day's events and special activities.

"Adventure Ocean" is a specially designed program for kids from 3 to 12 and teens from 13 to 17. Your children will find on-board pals in their age group: Aquanauts 3 - 5; Explorers 6 - 8; Voyagers 9 - 12; and Navigators 13 - 17. Children are always supervised by a professional certified youth staff member.

"Aquanauts" is for toilet-trained children ages 3 to 5. Activities include: Story time, face painting, dress-up days, building blocks, ring toss, art sculptures, Bingo, obstacle races, sing-alongs and more.

"Explorers" 6-8 years old and Voyagers 9-12 activities include Scattergories, Movies, Pizza Parties, Trashcan Art and Crazy T-Shirt Graffiti, Shuffleboard, Ping Pong, Basketball, Ring Toss, Obstacle Courses, Golf Putting and Wacky Races. Voyagers 9-12 also enjoy Tattoo Time & Cheek Art and scavenger hunts.

Navigators 13 to 17 can pursue their won agenda in the teen disco (restricted to those under 18) and Prom Night, Sailaway Socials, Karaoke, Volleyball Beach Parties and Video Game Tournaments. Sporting events include Basketball Tournaments, Fun Fitness Walk-a-thons, Golf Putting and more.

Resources: books
Cruise Vacations with Kids,
   Revised 2nd Edition, Stapen, Candyce H., 1999, Prima Publishing; ISBN: 0761516964

Have Grandchildren, Will Travel. Pilot Books, (800) 79-PILOT.

Travel for the Disabled

• Cruise ship accessibility and the Americans with Disabilities Act (ADA).

• *Resources*: travel organizations, agencies and publications specializing in travel for the disabled.

54-million physically challenged
Americans with $177 million in buying
power and a yen for travel give cruise
lines significant motive to improve
on-board accessibility.

What makes a cruise accessible?

Accommodating the disabled traveler goes way beyond ramps and rails. True accessibility demands adjustments and improvements in ship design and equipment; plus adequate staff training.

Cruise ships have come a long way with improvements to stateroom and bathroom layout: widened doorways, increased space between beds and furnishings, lowered bath countertops and easier-to-use faucets, light switches and door handles. Showers and toilets are somewhat more accessible with added grab rails, pull-down shower seats and bathroom doors that open outward.

The industry has a way to go to improve accessibility in public areas and is working to make shipboard activities and shore excursions more accessible.

Does the Americans with Disabilities Act (ADA) apply to cruise ships?

Most cruise lines operate in international waters and are registered in non-US countries. Historically, cruise lines abide by admiralty and maritime laws - not the laws that traditionally govern the United States. A Miami federal judge ruled that the American Disabilities Act (ADA) does not apply to any foreign-flagged cruise ships, exempting all but U.S. flagged ships from compliance. The United States Department of Transportation (DOT) has not yet implemented regulations governing accessibility standards for US- flagged commercial vessels.

Who is working on accessibility issues?

The International Council of Cruise Line, (ICCL) consists of the 17 largest passenger cruise lines that call on major ports in the US and abroad. ICCL's mission is to participate in the regulatory and policy development process and ensure that all measures adopted provide for a safe, secure and healthy cruise ship environment.

ICCL representatives are involved in the Passenger Vessel Advisory Committee (PVAC) which deals with accessibility onboard and onto new passenger vessels. The ICCL was also active in the International Maritime Organization,(IMO) working group that prepared passenger vessel guidelines which address design and operation features for elderly and disabled accommodations.

ICCL, 1211 Connecticut Avenue, Suite 800, Washington, DC 20036 (202) 296-8463, Fax:(202) 296-1676 [http://www.iccl.org/index2.html]

Highlights of cruise line efforts to accommodate disabled or impaired guests.

Royal Caribbean International can accommodate special needs, including:
- guests requiring wheelchairs
- visual impairments (including those that require service dogs)
- most special diets
- oxygen therapy (liquid oxygen, compressed gas oxygen or oxygen concentrator)
- dialysis (Continuous Ambulatory Peritoneal Dialysis only.)

For details on accessibility ask your travel agent for Royal Caribbean's *Accessible Seas* brochure. This guide includes stateroom and public area accessibility with the number and size of accessible staterooms on each of the line's 11 ships, width of doorways, turning radiuses and bathroom amenities, as well as a three-dimensional diagram of a stateroom layout.

Onboard medical care is detailed, along with features for the hearing impaired; transportation between the airport and the pier; and ports requiring tenders from ship to pier.

NCL's "Little Norway" tender vessel can come aside the ship's gangway doors, allowing wheelchairs to glide easily on and off!

Holland America Line

HAL's newest ships offer easy on-and-off's for wheel-chair travelers, making shore excursions a snap.

Able-bodied companions required?

Physically-challenged or wheelchair travelers should consult their travel agent regarding the cruise line's policies on able-bodied companions.

Can Rover Come Over?

Cruise line policies on seeing-eye, helper or companion dogs vary. Contact the cruise line early and work closely with your travel agent.

Visit CLIA at www.cruising.org for a guide to wheel-chair accessibility on a variety of ships.

Resources:

Agencies specializing in travel for the disabled.

Physically handicapped travelers

Able to Travel, 247 N. Main Street, Suite 308, Randolph, MA 02368 (800) 557-2047.

Access for Travel, 1429 10th Street West, Kirkland, Washington 98033, (425) 828-4220.

Flying Wheels Travel, PO Box 382, 143 West Bridge Street, Owatonna, MN 55060, (800) 535-6790.

The Society for the Advancement of Travel by the Handicapped ("SATH"), 347 Fifth Avenue, New York, New York 10016, (212) 447-7284

Yates Travel, 205 East 63rd Street, New York, New York 10021 (212) 758-1498.

Visually-impaired travelers

Accessible Tours / Directions Unlimited, 720 North Bedford Road, Bedford Hills, New York 10507, (914) 241-1700, (800) 533-5343.

Hearing-impaired travelers

Beasley Travel, Inc. Toll Free (877) 423-2753, Relay (800) 955-8770, [http://www.beasleytravel.com]
Beasley Travel offers a full line of cruises and tours

for the deaf and hearing. Their Annual Deaf &
Hearing Family Cruise provides interpreters and tour
guides and attracts more than 300 participants.

Herbtours, 9420 Elmbrook Court, Las Vegas,
Nevada, 89134-7802, TDD (702) 228-0556, fax (702)
228-3407.
Cruises and tours for the deaf and hearing-
impaired, always with a sign-language interpreter.

Travelers needing special medical assistance
Dialysis Traveler / Dialysis At Sea, 801 West Bay
Dr., Largo, FL 33770, (800) 544-7604, (727) 518-7311.
[http://www.dialysis-at-sea.com].
Dialysis at Sea books cruises for people on hemo-
dialysis or C.A.P.D. (Continuous Ambulatory
Peritoneal Dialysis) and C.C.P.D.. Cruises are accompanied by a board certified nephrologist, dialysis
nurse, and technicians.

National Oxygen Travel Service, 4600 Springboro
Pike, Dayton, OH 45439, (800) 862-NOTS, (937) 848-
6029.
Arranges for medical equipment to be delivered to
your cruise ship.

resources: magazines
Subscribe to SATH's quarterly publication, *Access
to Travel*, P.O. Box 352, Hawley Lane, New Baltimore,
New York 12124 (518) 731-9701.

Whitecaps without Nitecaps.

Travelers interested in the fellowship of recovering alcoholics will find meetings discreetly listed in daily activity programs. Alcoholics Anonymous meetings are often held in chapels, conference rooms and private staterooms. Ask the purser or guest services manager.

GAY & LESBIAN TRAVELERS

Resources: Agencies, tour operators, newsletters
RSVP Vacations

RSVP charters entire ships and resorts and transforms them into a gay and lesbian vacation escape. This well-established company supplements the ship's staff with their own crew; and has operated over 200 charter events.

Large ship cruises - This is RSVP's "main event," and there is often a waiting list. The company offers an average of two itineraries annually, such as a 7-day Mardi Gras cruise, with an overnight aboard ship in New Orleans at the height of Mardi Gras; and a 10-day Acapulco voyage. RSVP's large ship cruises have special entertainment, their own professional DJ, and a wide variety of shipboard activities including dances, theme parties, commitment ceremonies and guest speakers.

Small ship cruises - Offered three to four times yearly, these cruises are a smaller laid back version of the large ship cruises. These vacations are more port-intensive, with voyages to such locales as the French and Italian Riviera.

Family Abroad

Winner of the Out & About's Editor's Choice for "high-quality, high-value travel experience customized for the gay market."

Family Abroad's mission is to help gay men and

women thoroughly enjoy their travels by providing a gay-friendly and gay-sensitive travel environment, offering congenial companionship and a relaxed sense of traveling with people of similar sensibilities. The company supplies both first-class touring programs and leisurely travel experiences which focus on the scenery, culture, art and history of the destination.

Resources: Agencies and tour operators

Atlantis Events
   (310) 281-5450, (800) 628-5268

Family Abroad
   (800) 999-5500, [http://www.familyabroad.com]
   Order the Family Abroad Video, $5 including shipping. (800) 801-4771 Monday - Friday from 9 a.m. to 5 p.m. (MST).

Olivia Cruises and Resorts
   4400 Market Street, Oakland, CA 94608 (510) 655-0364, (800) 631-6277
   Charters small cruise ships for popular Greek Islands and Mediterranean cruises, exclusively for women.

RSVP Vacations
   (612) 379-4697, (800) 328-7787, [http://www.rsvp.net/]

Toto Tours
   (773) 274-TOTO, (800) 565-1241

Resources: Newsletters

Out & About, Inc., 8 West 19th Street, Suite 401, New York, NY 10011 (800) 929-2268, [http://www.outand-about.com].

For the latest information on travel opportunities for gays and lesbians, subscribe to the "Out & About" newsletter.

WEDDINGS & HONEYMOONS
• Cruise Chooser Honeymooners' Checklist

Convenience & Savings

Shipboard wedding can be done for a fraction of the cost of traditional weddings: have your wedding at the port of call or hold the ceremony aboard ship prior to departure. Consider having your guests attend the wedding and reception aboard ship, then return to shore and bid you Bon voyage as you set sail on your honeymoon. The most popular ports for weddings are Juneau, Alaska; Honolulu; Los Angeles; Miami; St. Thomas, USVI; Tortola, BVI; and Vancouver, BC.

Can we be married by the captain?

Ship's captains are not always authorized to perform marriage ceremonies. The bride and groom can be married by an officiate (notary public,) provided by the cruise line, or a minister, rabbi, priest or notary of their own choosing. Ask your travel agent.

Hot Tip: Ask your travel agent about cruises that depart on Sunday or Monday.

Chances are, your wedding date is set for a Saturday - and the last thing you need is the added stress of making it to the port on time.

"After a full wedding day, these newlyweds prefer to stay somewhere close to home their first evening together," observes Jack Chatham, vice-president of marketing and sales for Star Clippers.

More cruise lines are accommodating the bride and groom with Sunday and Monday sailings, such as late Sunday evening departures year-round on Caribbean voyages aboard the Star Clipper.

Can't Decide on a Wedding Gift?

Pamper Them

Newlyweds are often so overwhelmed with preparations for the big event that the best wedding present may be an opportunity to rest, relax and rejuvenate. Spa packages are an easy solution and welcome gift. Ask your travel agent about a pre-paid spa package including a massage, manicure, facial and hairstyle.

Spoil Them

Your travel agent or cruise reservationist can arrange for delivery of champagne, caviar and flowers to the honeymooner's stateroom. You'll need the newlywed's names, ship and sailing date.

Register 'em.

Ask your travel agent to set up a "bridal registry" where friends and family can put money towards a cruise, spa package or pre/post cruise stay-over.

Highlights of Wedding Packages

Carnival Cruise Lines

"Fun Ship" shoreside wedding packages are available in all of Carnival's continental U.S. home-ports and such beautiful ports as Ocho Rios, Key West, Nassau, San Juan, St. Thomas, Grand Cayman and Catalina Island. These all-inclusive packages include a civil ceremony, a decorated bridal aisle, a champagne toast with keepsake flutes, a wedding cake with topper, photography services and an engraved wedding announcement suitable for framing. Couples can also customize their wedding options with such value-added "extras" as post-ceremony receptions with open bar and hot and cold hors d'oeuvres, ice carvings, live music and videography services.

Crystal Cruises

Crystal Cruises offers Honeymoon, Anniversary and Renewal of Vows at Sea Packages. The Renewal of Vows at Sea program honors an anniversary with a special on board ceremony performed by the Captain or clergy. A bottle of Veuve Clicquot champagne, flowers, a portrait of the couple, and an anniversary cake for six-to-eight round out the package. The Crystal Anniversary Package includes champagne, a portrait and a miniature gold-plated clock with the line's seahorse logo. And for those spending their honeymoon aboard Crystal Harmony or Crystal Symphony, the Crystal Honeymoon Package offers champagne, sweetheart cake for two, a certificate signed by the Captain and a portrait.

Princess Cruises

Tie the knot aboard the Grand Princess, at the Hearts and Minds Wedding Chapel. The marriage ceremony is performed by the captain under the authority of the ship's registry (Bahamas, Panama, Liberia) Wedding packages start from $1,400 per couple and reception packages start from $70 per person. Options include a three-tiered wedding cake, hors d'oeuvres, music and official marriage certificate. Photography services are available through the ship's photographer and a Princess florist can design arrangements.

Tour Princess Cruises' Hearts and Minds Wedding Chapel online.
[http://www.princesscruises.com/onboard/wedding.html]

Royal Caribbean International

Royal Caribbean wedding coordinators are available to assist you with every aspect of your wedding day. Royal Caribbean now offers wedding ceremonies in Vancouver, British Columbia, New York, and Cape Canaveral, Fla., as well as Miami and St. Thomas, USVI. Weddings are performed in Miami by a notary public on embarkation day prior to sailing. You may also provide your own clergy to perform your ceremony. Legal ceremonies cannot be performed while at sea.

Wedding packages start at $800 and include bridal bouquet, boutonniere, marriage certificate, bottle of champagne, cake for two and a private photo session. RCI's Voyager of the Seas features a wedding chapel.

Royal Caribbean will allow up to 10 non-sailing guests to attend a wedding ceremony at no additional charge. If a reception is booked on the ship, additional guests may be allowed to attend.

Bridal couple must be sailing to hold a ceremony onboard a vessel and must book their cruise prior to booking their wedding package. Weddings may be booked up to four weeks prior to sailing, based on availability. Full payment for the wedding is due at the time of booking. The bridal couple is responsible for obtaining a valid marriage license. Royal Caribbean can assist in obtaining your marriage license through the mail.

Hot Tip: Please book early, since most cruise lines limit the number of ceremonies per sailing. It's recommended that the bridal party arrive at least one day prior to sailing to avoid late flights or traffic delays on their wedding day.

Honeymoons are Made of:

deluxe accommodations with a marble appointed bath and a double or queen-size bed; a candlelit table for two; just the two of you topside in moonlight, breakfast in bed, water-skiing, wind-surfing and Scuba diving, holding hands while wandering the exotic Bazaar of Istanbul, swimming with dolphins, stealing kisses under a Jamaican waterfall...

Honeymooners' Checklist

✔ Don't wait until the last minute, book your cruise and shipboard wedding 6-12 months in advance.

✔ Request a double or king-size bed at time of booking.

✔ Take advantage of the honeymooner package with complimentary champagne and cake, souvenir photos and special receptions.

B. **THE PERFECT STATEROOM**

Making cruise brochures, deck plans and 'virtual reality' work for you.
- Stateroom Convenience & Comfort Checklist
- Stateroom Use Checklist

Finding your home at sea is all about *location, location, location, location.*

    Location: inside Vs outside stateroom
    Location: forward Vs aft
    Location: highest to lowest deck
    Location: traffic and noise

When you price staterooms, remember that you are paying for convenience to activities, added amenities and prestige. Everyone has an equal opportunity to enjoy the cruise experience; from the fourth passenger in an bottom-deck inside stateroom; to the guest in the penthouse suite. Use the *Stateroom Convenience & Comfort Checklist* to find the perfect stateroom to meet your needs and standards.

Stateroom Categories

Fresh air and natural light determined prices on early passenger ships. Staterooms towards the top of the ship brought the highest price, while the cheapest passage was found 'down below' in dim, hot and stuffy lower decks. Moneyed travelers secured the best staterooms up top and those less fortunate spent their days topside, their nights in more affordable accommodations.

The 'modern' conveniences of electric lighting and in-room controlled air conditioning changed all that, but the traditional top-to-bottom category pricing structure remained. To get the most for your money on today's ships, decide what is important to you in terms of convenience, comfort, added amenities and prestige.

Checklist
Stateroom Convenience and Comfort

✔ **Location: Inside Vs Outside.**

Inside staterooms have no window. Outside or 'oceanview' have a porthole, picture windows, sliding glass doors or floor to ceiling windows.

✔ **Location: 'bow to stern.'**

Distance from stateroom to ship's front or back. Although most ships have "stabilizers" to minimize the motion of the ocean, the point of least motion is center ship.

✔ **Location: 'top to bottom.'**

How many decks away from the action is the stateroom? Is it convenient to the dining room, casino and pool? Are there elevators nearby?

✔ **Location: noise and traffic.**

The most popular staterooms are a distance from elevators and stairwells, discos, playrooms or gamerooms and laundry rooms. Consider the activity on the deck above the stateroom as well.

Making cruise brochures work for you: stateroom size and amenities.

Take comfort from the architectural renderings of sample staterooms found in many brochures. Think 'hotel' or resort and you'll be better able to imagine the size of your stateroom. Carefully review the brochure description.

Does the stateroom offer two twin beds or one queen? Are there recessed third and fourth beds? Is there sufficient closet/dresser space to stow your gear (Will you be bringing steamer trunks of cruise clothes? Sports or photography equipment? Dive gear? Strollers or wheelchairs?)

Now you can get *an inside stateroom with a view*, aboard Royal Caribbean International's Voyager of the Seas. It's a cruise ship first; some inside staterooms on Royal Caribbean International's Voyager of the Seas have bay windows overlooking the Royal Promenade, a horizontal atrium with great people-watching views of boutiques and restaurants.

Stateroom Use Checklist

How will you use your stateroom? Consider your plans when choosing your stateroom location.

✔ as a private rendezvous

✔ as a comfortable place to collapse after a full day

✔ for several daily outfit or 'costume' changes

✔ for family gatherings between trips to the pool

✔ as a quiet place for children's naps

✔ as a retreat for quiet time alone

✔ for parties and get-togethers

In addition to brochure sketches, many cruise lines offer stateroom virtual reality tours at their Web sites.

Visit these sites for a virtual tour of these ships.

Royal Caribbean International's Voyager of the Seas [http://www.rccl.com/voyageroftheseas/]

Holland America Line's Veendam [http://www.hollandamerica.com/vr/veendam_vr_index.html]

Princess Cruises' Grand Princess [http://www.princesscruises.com/fleet/grand/index.html]

Visit this site to view a video.
Radisson Seven Seas Navigator [http://www.streamingtravel.com/]

Also see the *Cruise Chooser CyberGuide.*

How Stateroom Categories Stack Up

One trend in newbuilds is to lower pre-fab 'layers' of staterooms into the ship's empty hull. Similar to stacking ice cube trays, lower and higher decks often have staterooms of similar or identical square footage. Lesser price category/ same square footage staterooms offer good value, despite less opulent furnishings and distance from the action. *(continued)*

Standard amenities usually include a bed or berth per passenger, private bathroom facilities with toilet, sink, tub or shower; closet and storage space, dresser or nightstand; temperature controls, radio/ TV and telephone.

Life Boats...

...can't sail without 'em- Can't see through 'em.

Life boats are good things - except when they block your view - carefully review deck plans to see where life boats are stored, and have your agent find out if your stateroom has an "obstructed view."

PART 3

The Best for Less

- ◆ Choosing and Using a Helpful Travel Agent

- ◆ Three Trends That Will Save You Money

- ◆ **Top 25** Bargains - Discounts - Deals

"It comes down to the way the American public is buying - they're buying discounts." Cruise line vice president sales & marketing.

Cruises have never been cheaper -- or more confusing -- to buy.

Consumers have been trained, by the cruise lines themselves, to shop for the best fares and to never, never pay retail. How can you make sense of the hodgepodge of deals, discounts and so-called special offers? First, find a savvy travel agent to do the footwork. Next, take advantage of three money-saving sales trends and 25 popular discount programs.

A. Choosing and Using a Helpful Travel Agent

"If one is going to spend hundreds or thousands of dollars, as well as a good chunk of valuable leisure time, it makes great sense to use a professional," Joseph Watters, president, Crystal Cruises.

It's that simple. You'll save time and money by using a qualified travel agent. Look for an agent who spends a majority of their time booking cruises. You can depend on expert advice from agents who are members of one or more of these professional associations.

To find a professional cruise counselor in your area contact these associations. (Have your city, zip code/postal code ready.)

Cruise Counselor Shopping Directory

American Society of Travel Agents (ASTA)
   Tel: 800-275-2782   [http://www.astanet.com]
Association of Retail Travel Agents (ARTA)
   Tel: 888-ARTA-NOW [http://www.artahdq.com]
Cruise Lines International Association (CLIA)
   Tel: 212-921-0066   [http://www.cruising.org]
Institute of Certified Travel Agents (ICTA)
   Tel: 800-542-4282   [http://www.icta.com]
National Association of Cruise Oriented Agents
(NACOA)
   Tel: 305-663-5626   [http://www.nacoa.com]

So many cruise lines - so little time...

*How an agent with "preferred suppliers" can get you
a better deal:*

Smart agents don't know everything about every
ship - they don't need to. The sharpest agents work
exclusively with a handful of cruise lines, usually one
or two companies from each cruise product type:
economy, expedition or adventure, mass-market, mid-
priced, premium and luxury.

This 'preferred-supplier' relationship allows agents to
really get to know each line's best values in accommodations, entertainment, dining options, itineraries and
shore excursions.

Lower prices for you!

Top-selling agencies can earn bonus commissions from
their preferred supplier. They pass these on to you as
cash rebates or incentives.

What can an agent do for you? They've got "pull" and they're in-the-know!

A superior travel agent will:

• Free up hours of your time for fun tasks such as shopping for cruise fashions or choosing your shore excursions.

Travelers who say, 'I'll just book it myself,' under-estimate the complexity of travel planning. One quick phone call by a cruise counselor can save you time and money. A qualified agent can cut through the red tape via agent-only telephone numbers or 'real-time' Internet booking engines. While you're on hold or in eternal download mode, a savvy travel agent can customize your vacation and cut costs.

• Share 'hands-on' experience and expertise: a qualified cruise agent has attended cruise line training seminars, earned a 'cruise counselor certifi-cation,' toured the ship, sailed with the cruise line or heard pros and cons from previous customers. She can often give you a thorough account of the level of service, entertainment and dining and keys to the perfect stateroom.

• Listen to you - hear your vacation likes and dislikes. Review your *Cruise Chooser Personality Quiz* results with your agent, so she can match your vacation personality with not only 'what's on sale,' but the very best vacation for you.

• Negotiate in your best interest. They've got 'pull': their sales records with preferred suppliers help them get you a better price.

• Handle all details. Your agent can help you choose the cruise line, ship, stateroom type, dining-room seating time, menu requests and air transportation (cruise line air/sea rate or frequent flyer savings.)
    She will research and book your pre - and post-cruise stayovers and on-board services such as shore excursions or spa packages. Your agent is also the best source for travel insurance and information on required immunizations and documentation.

• Make arrangements: A cruise counselor can easily arrange parties, weddings, reunions or conferences. She can also make arrangements for travelers with disabilities.

• Get you the goods: An agent who has a preferred supplier relationship with several cruise lines can get you cabin upgrades, added amenities and other extras. A 'top-producing' travel agent always has a better shot of seating you at the Captain's Table.

• Get you the best deal: A good travel agent is in-the-know; they get exclusive discounts, upgrades and special offers; they're the first to hear about deals and discounts. A top-producing agent can get you deals with their preferred supplier cruise line that you won't find elsewhere.

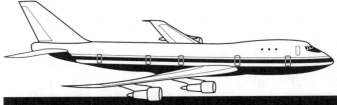

Airline Commission Cuts
Travel agencies to charge travel planning fees

How travel agents are paid.

If you've seen the headlines - you know that times 'they are a changin' for travel agents. The travel agent as 'order-taker' has gone the way of T-rex, this is the age of the travel sales consultant. Whether your agent earns straight commissions or charges a consultation fee, you're likely to get a better cruise vacation value with their help.

Internet Mega Agency
1-800 Cruise Broker
or Our Town Travel Shoppe?

Do 1-800 cruise agencies sell for less? Will you get better service with a local shop? Do online agencies offer personal service?

Who you choose to work with depends on your experience with planning a cruise vacation. Seasoned cruisers purchasing their fourth cruise may not need the same depth of service or interaction as first-timers. If you plan to sail again with a favorite cruise line and simply need to buy a ticket, you may not need much attention from an agent.

First-time cruisers, families with children, folks planning special events (reunions, weddings), and disabled travelers have a lot to gain by working face-to-face with a local agent. Long-distance travel agencies also offer personal consultation and cruise planning and several online agencies feature "live" operator assistance via "instant messaging" or telephone.

> Top online travel agencies spend more than $20 million per year on marketing.

B. These Three Trends in Cruise Sales Can Save you Money! (New ways cruises are sold.)

Until recently, building a customer base and setting cruise prices has been the job of the cruise companies. Consumers identified with Carnival, Royal Caribbean or Princess rather than ABC Cruise Shoppe, or GottaCruise.com. Customer "affiliation" or loyalty was with the producer of the cruise; the cruise line; rather than the distributor.

This is changing at the top of the market, argues cruise expert Wendy Determan, former columnist for *Leisure and Travel News*. Determan tells of an emerging new breed of travel agency, one with brand recognition equal to or greater than the 'household name' status of the cruise lines.

As this new breed of large retailers, travel agency consortia and online auction services dominate transactions; they will gain more power over terms and pricing.

Will the price of your next cruise be based on what the market can bear rather than the cruise companies' complex discounts, brochure rates and rebates?

1 *Travel consortia and mega-agencies purchase blocks of cruises at net rates, add their markup and market their own cruise vacation packages.*

www.window shopper or buyer?

Web sites alone don't really sell, argue top travel agency execs.

Joe Vittoria, president of The Travel Company wants to change that. He has backed his company's online booking tool Cruise Control with the consolidated sales power of dozens of cruise agencies. The Travel Company's online presence plus sales-savvy agents gives this conglomerate extra leverage in negotiating price, packages and commissions. (The Travel Company/Travel Services International.) [http://www.mytravelco.com]

www.vacation.com

AURA, Crown Travel Group, GEM-Cruiselink, GEM Canada, SPACE, TAN, TIME - you name it, if it's a travel agency consortium, Vacation.com is interested. Vacation.com has aquired these consortia, giving it as many as 9,4000 brick and mortar locations. The vision? Create a 'nationally branded leisure agency marketing powerhouse.' Preferred suppliers include Carnival, Crystal, Celebrity, Holland America, First European, Norwegian Cruise Line, Norwegian Coastal Cruises, Orient, Premier, Princess, Royal Caribbean and Windstar.
[http://www.vacation.com]

Chomp! Clicks and Bricks and Global Distribution Systems, Oh My!
Global distribution system (GDS), Amadeus has aquired Vacation.com, in a deal worth $90 million. Amadeus also has a technology and marketing partnerships with consortia Action 6 and MAST and franchises Travelbyus and Uniglobe. Highlights: More technology for travel agents: 'Amadeus Cruise' is a graphical booking tool for travel agents featuring cruises from Royal Caribbean International, Celebrity Cruises and Princess Cruises.

2 Cruise companies sell inventory direct to the consumer via:

- online booking engines
- direct marketing
- Single brand stores (which operate much like car dealerships, selling only one make.)
- shipboard single-brand travel agent.

Online booking engines.

At a recent Seatrade Cruise Shipping Convention, cruise executives debated the Internet's impact on cruise marketing. While a majority of cruise companies have consumer Web sites, they continue to rely on travel agents for distribution of the cruise product. A few now sell direct to the consumer with online reservations and booking capabilities.

Carnival Cruise Lines has launched Fun Online®, the cruise industry's first 'real-time' Internet booking engine for consumers.

Site Highlights: information on every vessel in the "Fun Ship" fleet, deck plans, ship descriptions and stateroom descriptions; cruising areas, itineraries and sailing dates. Pricing information is provided for both cruise-only and air/sea with rates broken down by stateroom accommodation level. SSL-encrypted credit card online payment.
[http://www.carnival.com/consumers/welcome.asp]

Direct marketing: Visitors to cruise line Web sites can

register for direct mail or e-mail about cruise specials. Renaissance Cruises and other companies sell direct by tagging television advertisements with the cruise line reservation telephone number.

Single-brand stores and shipboard travel agents. Guests aboard Carnival Cruise Lines' Fun Ships can purchase their next cruise from a shipboard Carnival agent. Carnival Vacation Stores sell Carnival, Holland America Line, Cunard Line, Seabourn Cruise Line, Costa Cruises and Windstar.)

3 *Online bidding services sell cruises as a commodity product.*

These cyber-shops function much like the brick and mortar consolidators or bucket shops, selling cruise inventory on a space-available basis.

Cyber Shops

Travelocity
[http://www.travelocity.com] has surpassed 10 million registered members and has served more than 1 million customers.

Yahoo!
Yahoo! travel is actually a 'co-brand' of Travelocity/Preview Travel. This portal partnership brings travel deals to your desktop.

C. **THE BEST FOR LESS**
Bargains, Discounts,Deals

25 DISCOUNT PROGRAMS
Where can you find these money-saving
discounts?
- your local newspaper: Sunday travel section.
- cruise line & travel Web sites.
- cruise and travel magazines.
- travel newsletters.
- a travel agent.

This guide explains how these popular discount
programs work. Examples are valid at time of publication.

For current pricing and special offers go to:
www.cruisechooser.com and register for the
Cruise Chooser E- Mail Deal Newsletter

---

25 Discount Progams to Save You Money!

1) 2-FOR -1
   2nd PERSON SAILS FREE
   3rd & 4th PERSON FREE

2) AIR ADD-ONS DISCOUNT or FREE AIR

3) ALUMNI/PAST PASSENGER

4) BACK TO BACKS

5) CHILDREN'S DISCOUNTS

6) CRUISE ONLY

7) EARLY BOOKING DISCOUNTS

8) E-MAIL ALERT

9) FLORIDA RESIDENT/FLORIDA VISITOR

10) FREE DAYS/NIGHTS

11) GROUP RATE

12) HOLIDAY CRUISES

13) INTRODUCTORY CRUISES

14) MATURE TRAVELER DISCOUNTS

15) ONBOARD SPENDING CREDITS

16) ONLINE CRUISE AUCTIONS

17) ORGANIZATIONAL DISCOUNTS

18) PRE & POST STAYOVERS

19) REBATE OR INCENTIVE

20) REPOSITIONING CRUISE

21) SEASONAL & SHOULDER SEASON SAVINGS

22) STANDBY & 'PIER HEAD JUMP'

23) TIE-INS

24) TOUR CONDUCTOR

25) UPGRADE

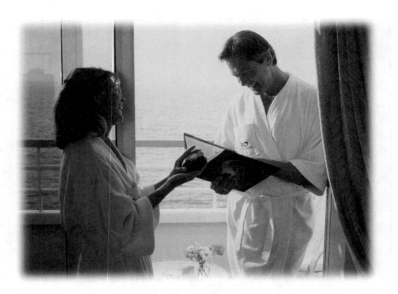

1. BUY THE NUMBERS
2-FOR -1
2nd PERSON SAILS FREE
First person pays 'full price' plus port charges and airfare.
Second person sails for free, plus port charges and airfare.

Example:
Crystal Cruises
Crystal Cruises offers Up To 2-for-1 savings with fares from $1,345 per person for category "G". Port charges of $95 to $110 /person included. Low air add-ons available.

3rd & 4th PERSON FREE
First and Second guests pay 'full price' plus port charges and airfare.
Third & Fourth guests pay only airfare and port charges.

Four's a Crowd?

Consult your travel agent and pay close attention to stateroom dimensions and layout. Most staterooms are very comfortable for two people and their luggage. Consider packing lean and light to accommodate luggage for four. A third and fourth adult plus luggage can cramp everyone's style.

Kids will enjoy the adventure of pull-down/recessed beds. Although daytime might find them napping in your bed. Before you invite two more friends, refer to your results from the *Cruise Chooser Personality Quiz* & see the *Stateroom Use Checklist*.

2. AIR ADD-ONS/AIR DISCOUNT

Take advantage of cruise line 'block' fares. Air lines reserve a quantity of seats on specific flights for cruise passengers, often at reduced rates. Ground transportation from airport to the cruise port is usually included.

Examples:
Carnival Cruise Lines
Select sailings on Jubilee departing from Miami on Sunday & Wednesday; 10 days to the Panama Canal

Rates from only $949 Including port charges. Plus air for only $99! - from select gateway cities.

Radisson Seven Seas Cruises

On select sailings, RSSC offers free round-trip Business Class air or an extra $1,000 savings for those who decline the Business Class air offer.

3. ALUMNI/PAST PASSENGER

Most major cruise lines offer special alumni newsletters with exclusive reduced fares, coupons and extra incentives to sail again.

Examples:

Crystal Cruises' Exclusive Crystal Society Savings & Benefits

- Additional 5% savings for reservations made during your cruise.
- Crystal Society Membership Card.
- Complimentary subscription to Society News.
- Special onboard parties and activities plus an exclusive photo session with your captain on all designated Crystal Society Sailings.
- Priority check-in at the pier on all cruises.
- Complimentary bottle of wine and fresh flowers beginning with your tenth cruise.

Disney Cruise Line's Castaway Club

Your complimentary membership features a number of special privileges, including:

Select offers on future sailings • Disney Insider newsletter featuring updates on Walt Disney World® and Disney Cruise Line happenings • Special onboard recognition during your next cruise • members-only Toll-free reservation and information line.

P & O Cruises' P.O.S.H. Club

P & O started the P.O.S.H. Club exclusively for repeat passengers.

Advantages include:

• quarterly magazine.

• invitations to join P.O.S.H. Club holidays and party cruises at special rates.

• free shore excursions.

• wine and an exclusive gift.

• shipboard discounts for shopping, hairdressing and photo-processing.

• discounts on Avis car rental world wide.

Why P.O.S.H?

Posh actually derives from the days before air-conditioned ships. On cruises from Britain to India the best way to travel was Port Out, Starboard Home, ensuring you got the shady side of the ship in both directions.

Windstar Cruises' Foremast Club

Cruising with Windstar automatically enrolls you

in this complimentary club. Benefits include 2-for-1 savings on select cruises • special discounts • invitations to onboard events such as special receptions with the Captain.

4. BACK TO BACKS

East meets West, Caribbean that is. Back to back savings are most often available on ships that alternate between Eastern and Western Caribbean cruises. Book both itineraries consecutively and save up to 30% off your ticket.

5. CHILDREN'S DISCOUNTS

Kids always sail for less as 3rd or 4th guests in a cabin. Also look for 'children sail free' or 'grandchildren cruise free' (3 & 4th passengers in stateroom sailing with two full-fare passengers). Reduced children's rates usually do not include airfare or port charges. Look for 'free airfare for kids' and 'kids under X age sail free'. Ages 2 and under often sail for free with two full-fare passengers.

Example:
American Hawaii Cruises
Children 2-17 years, sharing cabin with two full-fare passengers sail Free. Children under 2 cruise free.

6. CRUISE ONLY

Originally offered for guests living within driving range of cruise ports, you save by driving or using frequent flyer mileage for your airfare. Hot Tip: When you purchase your own airfare, consider buying a non-refundable ticket Vs refundable. Purchase from 45 to 7 days before departure and save as much as 50 percent over a refundable fare. Any fee for changing your ticket; should you need to cancel completely; is worth your savings. Ask the airline or your travel agent about flight-change fees and whether the price of your ticket can be applied to a future flight.

7. E-MAIL SALES ALERTS

Go to www.cruisechooser.com and register with participating cruise lines for E-mail Sales Alerts.

Examples:

Join **Windjammer's** CyberSailor Internet Club and you'll receive and 10-day advance notice of available cabins for each of their ships - and receive up to a 50% discount on those last minute bookings! (discount applies to new bookings only) Or, if you prefer, Windjammer will notify you each Friday via E-mail.

Join **Delta Queen Steamboat's** E-mail List - whenever they have specials they'll drop you an e-mail.

8. EARLY BOOKING DISCOUNTS

Early-booking discounts apply to cruises booked 3-9 months in advance.

Examples:

Holland America Line

HAL "reduced pricing" increase early booking savings from 25 percent to 43-48 percent

Costa Cruises

Save up to $1,700 per couple with Costa Cruises' Andiamo rates. Book at least 90 days in advance.

Radisson Seven Seas Cruises

Song of Flower offers Extended Early Booking Savings of $300-$900 per person, plus free round-trip Business Class air on the select sailings in the Far East/ Indian Ocean and Red Sea/Mediterranean.

9. FLORIDA RESIDENT/VISITOR

Floridian discounts were the original cruise-only fares. These special fares are also offered at the last minute on undersold sailings. Consider adding an all-inclusive cruise to your next Florida vacation.

VIP TIPS

5 reasons to be invited to dine with the Captain.

1. Rich

Big spenders and guests in the most expensive staterooms are always welcome

2. Famous

What makes you famous? Purple Heart, Congressional Medal of Honor, Pulitzer Prize Inventor, Corporate Big-Wig, Successful Entrepreneur, Politician, Sports, Arts or Music Celebrity?

3. Talented
Are you a good story-teller? World traveler? Do you have a tale of adventure-tragedy-success? Have you experienced a dramatic event and lived to tell about it?

4. Frequent Sailor
Alumni cruisers are always welcome.

5. Lucky
Heck, there's always a chance for pleasant, well-meaning folk to find a seat.

Hot Tip: *The formal night fills up first. Ask your travel agent to request an invitation.*

10. FREE DAYS/NIGHTS
To calculate actual savings, compare the per diem or daily rate to the full fare with airfare included.

11. GROUP RATE - Travel agency buys block space of eight or more staterooms in advance and passes the volume saving on to you. You pay the lower rate but don't have to travel as a group. Group booking benefits with **Commodore Cruise Line** include a bottle of champage or chocolate-covered strawberries in each berth; one group photo per stateroom; stateroom upgrades, group parties and one tour conductor berth per 15 passengers. (see tour conductor, below.)

12. HOLIDAY CRUISES

Holiday discounts make starting a new family tradition - a holiday cruise - easy and affordable. You and your loved ones can celebrate in style and save money. Usual seasonal discount period: Two weeks before Christmas.

Example:
Holland America Line

2-for-1 fares on Holiday Cruises - up to 61 percent off six sailings during the holiday season. Plus additional discounts of up to $250.

13. INTRODUCTORY CRUISES

(Inaugural seasons, new itineraries)

We won't enter a market unless we can dominate it!" says a Carnival Cruise Lines executive.

With 62 new ships coming in the next five years; and as current ships move to new ports of departure, watch for introductory pricing and 'grand-opening' specials. Save as much as 30%.

Examples:
Cunard

Join the Caronia on her inaugural season in the Amazon. Sail for 6, 8 or 14 Day segments. Cruise sails from Fort Lauderdale, FL to Manaus, Brazil. Visit St. Croix, USVI , Antigua, Guadeloupe, Barbados, French Guiana, and the Brazilian ports of Santarem, Alter do Chao, Parintins.

Royal Caribbean International

Sail the Explorer of the Seas' Inaugural season of 7 night Eastern Caribbean voyages starting at
$ 799 per person.

14. MATURE TRAVELER DISCOUNTS

Go ahead, You've earned it! Discounts usually begin at age 55.

Example:

Norwegian Cruise Line

Travelers over 55 can take advantage of NCL Senior Rates; for example: 7-Day Caribbean Cruise onboard the Norway. Departs Round-trip Miami to: St. Maarten, St. John/ St. Thomas and NCL's Private Island. Cruise Only Rates Starting from: (Prices Include Port Charges) Inside Stateroom: $549 Oceanview Stateroom: $599

Rates listed are per person, including port charges, based on double occupancy and for 1st and 2nd guest. At least one guest in the stateroom needs to be 55 years or older.

15. ONBOARD SPENDING CREDITS

Spending credits, casino credits, discount coupons for purchases in the giftshop, boutique or spa. Ask your travel agent about alumni passenger spending credits and promotional coupons.

Example:
Crystal Cruises

Crystal Cruises offers Crystal CruiseBank with special onboard spending credits from $250/person.

16. ONLINE CRUISE AUCTIONS

The explosion of travel auctions sites illustrates a shift in pricing power from cruise line to retailer and consumer. Bargain shoppers with flexible schedules can take advantage of clearance sale prices as online auctions sell last-minute vacancies and "distressed inventory" or low-occupancy sailings.

A reminder: auction prices do not automatically equal value or the best deal. Avoid getting 'carried away' in the frenzy of a spirited auction. Carefully review the site's rules and policies - before you start packing!

Many auction sites work within a bidding period of between one and 14 days, and maintain a minimum bid or reserve. If the unspecified minimum is not reached, the cruise is withdrawn from sale.

Auction Action:

Do your homework

- What is basis of the discount - some sites claim to sell at rates as much as 65% off retail - but what is retail? retail brochure rate?

• *What is included?* airfare and transfers from airport to cruise port? land transportation from home to cruise port? port charges? ticket processing or delivery charges?

• *Know from whom you're buying* - deal only with affiliates of clearly identified, established cruise lines and compare local travel agent's prices for the same cruise package.
[http://www.auctionwatch.com]
Auction Watch is a consumer site dedicated to ethical auction practices.

Contact the American Society of Travel Agents (ASTA) 800-275-2782
Ask if the auction site/affiliated travel retailer is recommended by ASTA.

• *Secure your transaction*- Pay by credit card and only trade with sites that support secure socket layer or other encryption formats Netscape Navigator alerts users to secured transaction sites. You can also check security by clicking on "page source" under "view" on your toolbar.

Resources: **Sample Auction Web Sites**

[http://www.adventurebid.com]   [http://www.priceline.com]
[http://www.allcruiseauction.com] [http://www.reallycheapfares.com]
[http://www.bid4vacations.com]   [http://www.travelbids.com]
[http://www.luxurylink.com]   [http://www.travelzoo.com]

17. ORGANIZATIONAL DISCOUNTS

Don't forget your membership benefits from AAA; AARP; credit unions; professional associations such as the Florida Bar, Plumbers and Steamfitters Union, Your County Teacher's Association, university alumni associations, corporate employee benefits departments, religious affiliations, civic or environmental organizations such as Shriner's, Center for Marine Conservation, etc.

World Ocean & Cruise Liner Society

New features and benefits include:

- $25 per person onboard credit on Holland America or Windstar.

- $100 per stateroom onboard credit on Radisson Seven Seas.

- 12 monthly issues of *Ocean & Cruise News*.

- Access to Ocean & Cruise News Web site.

World Ocean & Cruise Liner Society, PO Box 92, Stamford, CT 06904. (203) 329-2787

18. PIER-HEAD JUMP/STANDBY RATES

Named for sailors who caught their ship at the very last minute as it pulled away from the pier. Last minute deals on undersold sailings can be found as far out as 6 to 8 weeks before departure date. If you are flexible with your vacation schedule and don't mind a limited choice of stateroom style and location; the savings are significant!

19. PRE- and POST- Cruise Stayovers

Consider adding a few extra days to your vacation for a pre-or post-cruise stayover. Many cruise lines reserve blocks of rooms in port city hotels so you can stay for less. You've already paid the airfare; why not take advantage of the cruise line's hotel package? Enjoy some bonus rest and relaxation or go exploring! Most cruise line stayovers include transportation from airport to hotel to cruise port. Ask if the deal includes escorted tours, local attraction coupons or tickets, meals or rental cars. Your agent may also be able to recommend an alternative package.

Example:

Radisson Seven Seas Cruises

RSSC offers free round-trip economy airfare from 79 North American gateway cities or a three-night deluxe hotel stay at the Le Meridien Hotel in Tahiti prior to their seven-night voyage in Polynesia.

20. REBATE OR INCENTIVE

Top producing agencies offer you a percentage of their commission - in cash or goodies such as onboard spending credits, discount coupons, wine or fruit in your stateroom or a stateroom category upgrade.

21. REPOSITIONING CRUISE

As seasons change, ships follow the sun from one region to another. Ships are repositioned when new ships and new itineraries are introduced. Ships that winter in the Caribbean may traverse the Panama Canal to summer in Alaska, and return south in fall. Repositioning cruises naturally offer more days at sea and are often 7- to 10 nights or longer. Off-season rates plus offbeat itineraries including transatlantic crossings make repositioning cruises a great bargain.

Examples:

Cunard

Southern Crossing onboard the Caronia. 17 Days from Southampton to Fort Lauderdale, FL

Visiting Portugal, Barbados, Dominica, St. Kitts & Nevis, San Juan.

Princess Cruises

Mexican Riviera Repositioning onboard the Dawn Princess sails from Acapulco to Los Angeles. Priced from only USD $599 per person cruise only.

Royal Caribbean International

From $1199 Cruise Only Transatlantic Miami to Barcelona in April.

22. SEASONAL SAVINGS / SHOULDER SEASONS

Best times for seasonal savings:

Caribbean: September to Christmas, first and second week in January, April to June

Alaska: May and September

Bermuda: May and September

Europe: April, May September, October

Example:

Windstar Cruises

Andalusia & Provence - 7-Day Cruises on Wind Star - 35-40% Off (Cruise-only) September 3,17; October 1, 8, 15, 22 29; and November 5, 2000

BONUS: Round-trip air from New York to ship for $399pp!

23. TIE INS

Keep your eyes open for co-sponsored cruise discounts. You may find a deal on your next supermarket shopping trip or on your credit card statement!

Credit Card Discounts: Major credit card companies offer special discounts on select cruises.

Purchase your cruise with your credit card and receive onboard spending credits.

Example Product Promotions: Fox Video offered cruise savings in specially packaged videos. Nestles teamed its chocolate morsels with a **Disney Cruise Line** promotion. Elizabeth Arden launched a new perfume with a free cruise contest. Tic Tac Candies and **Windjammer Cruises** co-sponsored discounted sailings.

24. TOUR CONDUCTOR

One free for every 15! Leadership has its rewards, since most cruise lines allow one free 'tour conductor' for every 8 staterooms booked. (16 people total, 15 full fare, #16 sails for airfare + port charges.)

Some lines offer a complimentary tour conductor fare for every 10 guests or 5 staterooms booked. **Windstar Cruises** has offered one free tour conductor per every 10 guests plus a second tour conductor berth for $495 on seven-day Belize, Caribbean and Costa Rica cruises.

How to be the Best Pied Piper

Get enthusiastic and invite your friends, neighbors and associates to a special reception or cruise night with snacks, videos and brochures!

Ask your travel agent for supplies and support. See organizational discounts for examples of affinity groups.

25. UPGRADE

Another great reason to book early. Depending on how sold out the cruise is; you pay for a lesser priced stateroom category and are 'upgraded' to a pricier stateroom - at no additional cost!

Examples:

NCL

NCL offers a 2 stateroom category upgrade on every ship and every

itinerary throughout 2000.

Celebrity Cruises

Captain's Club (Alumni program) members receive an automatic one-category upgrade.

See our VIP TIPS *(found after Tip 9)* and discover how to be invited to dine at the Captain's Table.

PART 4

Cruising Made Easy

- ◆ Money Well Spent
- ◆ Service: Tip Guide
- ◆ Dining
- ◆ Celebrating Special Occasions
- ◆ What to pack/What to wear: Packing Guide
- ◆ Special Interest Theme Cruises
- ◆ Documents
- ◆ Insurance
- ◆ Health Tips
- ◆ Safety & Security

Cruise Chooser Checklists:
- ✔ What to Wear & Pack
- ✔ Getting your Passport
- ✔ Life boat drill

A. Money Well Spent

What is cash-less cruising? • Can I pay my bill by credit card? • How much cash should I bring? • Are ATMs available? • What does 'all-inclusive' include? • What expenses can I plan for?

What is cash-less cruising?

Many cruise lines operate on a no-cash-required 'tab' system. All purchases can be billed to your onboard account, which you pay at the end of your cruise.

Quick & Easy Account Setup

1. At the cruise terminal check-in counter: an imprint of your credit card will be made, and you'll be given a nifty shipboard charge card which often doubles as your stateroom key and passenger ID. Use it to pay for beverages, bar tabs, spa and salon services, souvenirs, shore excursions, baby-sitting, golf practice and other fun things.

2. Upon embarkation: Go to the purser's desk or guest relations center to set up your account.

3. In your stateroom: Several ships offer an interactive television service that allows you to make financial arrangements from your stateroom.

Can I pay my bill by credit card?

Quick & Easy Payment Options

You'll receive a statement of your bill on the last night of your voyage. Make any adjustments or corrections to your statement as soon as possible, and you'll avoid delays. Payment is due before disembarkation.

You can review your onboard expense report at any time.

1. Log on for an instant status report via your in-stateroom interactive TV.

2. Go to the purser's desk or guest relations center.

HOT TIP: Avoid the rush hour - right before disembarkation. Settle up early the last night or early on the final morning of your cruise. Leave the bill on your credit card for quick settlement.

Cash

How much cash should I bring?

Shipboard expenses: the only cash you'll need will be for the casino, shopping trips ashore and for tipping on the final day of your voyage. Everything can be billed to your account. In port: the US dollar is preferred as "hard currency" in many ports. You'll do well to have small US bills on hand, along with a small amount of local currency.

Exchange rate tip:

> To check the latest exchange rates visit the
> Universal Currency Converter Web site
> [http://www.xe.net/currency]

ATMs
Are ATMs available?

Save money and time by using an ATM. ATMs that accept bank cards linked to Visa's Plus and MasterCard Cirrus networks are available in dozens of countries; ports of call, airports and aboard some ships. Exchange rates are often better than those at exchange bureaus, although fees can be costly.

Before you leave home, ask your bank for a list of overseas locations of ATMs you can use. Call Cirrus ATM location number: 1-800-4-CIRRUS.

Important: You may need to establish a new Personal Identification Number, PIN for foreign travel. Also ask if there's a daily withdrawal limit or a surcharge on multiple withdrawals.

What does 'all-inclusive' include?

Most all-inclusive cruise fares include accommodations, on-board entertainment, travel to a variety of ports-of-call, on-board activities, all meals and non-carbonated, non-alcoholic drinks. A few lines have 'no tipping required' policies. Luxury lines include all beverages, extra amenities and a complimentary shore excursion.

What expenses can I plan for?

How do cruise lines manage to provide so much entertainment, food and activities for the price of your ticket? They make up the difference with income from bars, boutiques, salons, shore excursions, miscellaneous services and the casino.

> "We lose money on every account, but we make it up in volume." T.K.

Bar

Most ships charge for soda and alcoholic beverages. Coffee, tea, juice and lemonade are free. Drink prices are comparable to those at a resort or hotel bar. You can charge your tab to your shipboard account, and the cruise line will add 15% for gratuities.

Gambling/Gaming

gam'ble, v.t..

1. to bet, to wager

gam'ble, n. an act which depends on chance; a risk; an uncertain venture.

Gaming, gambling - whatever you call it, win or lose, there are no guarantees. Add some mad money to your cash supply for Lady Luck.

Let's go shopping!

Port lecturers pride themselves on providing a comprehensive yet entertaining look at ports of call. Favorite historical landmarks, natural wonders and popular shopping spots are highlighted along with current events and local festivals.

Most lecturers ask you to patronize retailers who advertise in shipboard magazines. These 'preferred' shops do usually offer large selection, convenient payment options, accessible entrances and sometimes - clean restrooms. The cruise line's recommendation does not automatically guarantee the best bargains.

Suzy Gershman has the inside track on shopping - worldwide and in Caribbean ports-of-call. Whether your mission is emeralds or macadamia nuts, Suzy's guides give you the secrets of successful shopping: *Frommer's Born to Shop Caribbean Ports of Call*, by Frommers, Suzy Gershman, 2nd edition, 1997, IDG Books Worldwide; ISBN: 0028607120.

Also see *Born to Shop London, Born to Shop France*...

Onboard Shopping

No need to wait 'till you're in port. Go ahead and blow your casino jackpot. It's time to splurge on that emerald ring or shimmering gold swimsuit. If you're after a bargain, however, do a bit of advance research on jewelry prices and luxury goods.

Money-Saver: Many ships have 'last chance' sales on merchandise towards the end of your voyage.

Unless you want to wear your ship's logo T-shirt while you're onboard, buy your souvenirs at the end of the cruise.

Money Saver: When you book your cruise, ask your travel agent about onboard spending credits or shopping coupons. Alumni or past passenger clubs often include coupons in their mailings or newsletters.

Photos

Gotta' have em? Ship's photographers are pros at capturing the essence of your cruise. One-of-a-kind photos - such as shaking the Captain's hand on formal night - are worth the $6 to $12. You're under no obligation to purchase photos from the ship's photography staff, however.

Videos are another fun way to show off to friends back home. Several lines offer "donut" videos: prefab footage of highlights of the ship and ports of call with personal shots of you and your party spliced in.

You'll also want to shoot your own, so bring plenty of film and batteries or disposable cameras. Remember to pack your video camera's battery charger, and extra tapes.

Money in your Pocket

Avoid paying "resort" prices for necessities. Pack extra film, video-tape, batteries, over the counter medications, sunscreen, feminine and baby supplies.

Art auctions

Look out big spenders! Know your subject and your budget before you bid. What a fun way to decorate, though, the work you acquire will make an great conversation starter and reminder of your cruise.

Shore Excursions

What to do next? Should we go shopping or hop a helicopter flight into the maw of a Hawaiian volcano - shore excursions vary greatly in experience and price, ranging from $30 to $250 per person. Whether you buy what the cruise line offers or shop around depends on your level of comfort and that of your traveling companions. You are paying for convenience and "a sure thing - no surprises."

It's no surprise that many cruise lines charge a premium for their pre-packaged shore excursions. The cruise lines have done their research and they offer hassle-free trips to the most sought-after, popular sites.

Novice travelers, families with small children or those in need of extra support (seniors, physically challenged) can easily take advantage of the cruise line packaged excursions.

If you're comfortable in your new surroundings, you might consider shopping ashore for organized tours or private guides. You can also arrange your own sightseeing by sharing a taxi or car rental with fellow passengers.

Spas

Ahh! Go ahead, treat yourself! For the best selection of times and services, reserve your salon and spa appointments the first day of your cruise. Take a moment to orient yourself to the spa and the menu of services; often a spa package is priced lower than the same services a-la-carte. Your travel agent may also be able to save you money with pre-paid spa packages.

Salon and spa personnel salaries are supplemented by tips and commissions on all product sales. Spa products do make wonderful souvenirs, but you are not obligated to purchase anything.

B. Tip Guide *"TIP: to insure promptness"*

Many employees, including your stateroom steward, bartender, masseuse, stylist, waiter and busboy -- count on tips as a significant part of their income. No ship requires you to tip employees although a 15% gratuity is automatically added to bar and wine bills at time of purchase.

A few cruise lines have policies of "no tipping required" where tips are accepted, though discouraged. Luxe lines with "gratuities not accepted" policies build tips into the price of your ticket. No tipping is expected.

How Much Do I Tip?

Ask your travel agent about recommended daily amounts or consult with the ship's purser. Many cruise lines provide 'suggested' tipping guidelines and envelopes on the last night of your cruise. Consult your travel agent before sailing, read the final pages of your cruise brochure or ask the purser.

Charge It!

Crystal Cruises, Disney Cruise Line and others allow you to charge tips to your shipboard account. You'll receive printed redeemable tip cards to sign and present to your waiters and stateroom steward.

Standard tipping guidelines:
    stateroom steward ($3-4 per day)
    dining room steward ($3-4 per day)
    assistant dining room steward ($1.50- $1.75 per day)
    bus boy ($1.50-2 per day)
    wine steward ($1 per bottle)
    butler ($2 per day)
    maitre d' (.75 per day)
    salon & spa staff 15-20% of service price

If you have received superior service - here's where to show your appreciation. Other personnel to remember: casino dealer, baby sitter and shore excursion guides. Officers, cruise staff and entertainers are never tipped.

What about tipping for service in open-seating or alternative/theme restaurants?
Since waiters in the casual or theme restaurants often differ from your assigned wait staff, we recommend $1 per person for casual settings and up to $4 per person for alternative restaurants aboard luxury ships.

Superior service is a hallmark of cruising and above average service should be rewarded. Whom to tip and how much is at your discretion.

C. Dining

Tips on making your dining reservations: first or second seating, number of tablemates, smoking or non-smoking.

Seating reservations allow for serving the entire ship without delays or crowds. Ships' galleys run like clockwork to serve up to 1000 passengers at a seating. Most ships offer two seatings for breakfast, lunch and dinner.

Typical seating times are:

First or Early Seating	2nd or Late Seating
Breakfast: 7 a.m. or 8 a.m.	8:30 a.m. or 9 a.m.
Lunch: Noon	1:30 p.m.
Dinner: 6 p.m. or 6:30 p.m.	8:15 p.m. or 8:30 p.m.

When making your seating time choice consider these four factors:
1. Your routine mealtimes at home.
2. Personal health requirements/restrictions.
3. Scheduled activities onboard.
4. Time spent ashore.

Your travel agent will make your seating arrangements in advance. These seating arrangements will be listed in your boarding documents and in your stateroom literature. Early seating is the most popular on Alaska cruises, Late seating on Caribbean and

Mediterranean. The early bird gets the worm, so book your cruise and make your dining reservations as far in advance as possible.

Whenever possible, be prompt for your scheduled dinner reservation. Being on time for breakfast and lunch is less critical, since there are many alternatives to the main dining room. You can order breakfast in bed or al fresco; on the Lido deck. Enjoy a casual midday buffet or try a local restaurant in port.

Choosing your table style (number of tablemates.) When making your seating time selection, you'll have a choice of the number of people at your table, usually 2,4,8,10 or 12.

What if you don't like your tablemates? Not a problem, ask the dining room manager for another table.

Get the most from your waiter. Let him know what you like and dislike early in the cruise. The dining room staff prides themselves on a smooth-running, satisfying dining experience. The best waiters anticipate your needs in advance, but aren't mind readers. Do you like decaf coffee after dinner? Steak blood-rare? Let the waiter know, and you'll enjoy the best service.

D. Celebrating Special Occasions

Susan and Tom celebrate their marriage each year with an anniversary cruise.

"We actually celebrate three anniversaries: Tom and I met at the wedding of Tom's sister and my brother. My sister met her husband at the same wedding. Our annual cruise is like a family reunion - with everyone from the nephews and nieces to grandparents.

On the first day-at-sea, my mother-in-law and all us ladies meet at the spa, where we catch up on family 'business.' I don't worry about everyone having a good time. My dad loves to dance and he's an expert on blackjack. And we can't keep Tom Sr., a retired chef, from the ship's galley tour.

It's been a great experience for my teenage nephews and nieces, too. Onboard ship they have just enough freedom to keep out of trouble - we'll find them at the pool, or in the disco.

Tom and I look forward to moonlight strolls topside and exploring ports of call by motorcycle."

Cruises are made for celebrations - anniversaries, family reunions, birthdays and weddings - what could be more fun and easy than a cruise?! Most cruise lines will treat you like a VIP and even throw in a complimentary cake to honor the occasion.

TIP: Make your plans at least three weeks in advance of your sailing date. For tips on weddings, see Part II The Perfect Cruise for You.

Ask your travel agent about planning a private party catered with champagne, flowers, canapés, wine and cheese. There are so many options aboard today's ships - bring your video camera to capture memories of your special celebration.

E. What to Wear/What to Pack:
Packing Checklist
What clothing will you need for your cruise?

It depends on your ship's:
• level of formality
• sailing date
• itinerary
• shore excursions

Royal Caribbean International offers basic packing guidelines for several cruise regions. Here are clothing suggestions for Alaska, Canada / New England, Caribbean, Bahamas, Bermuda, Mexico, Hawaii, Panama Canal and Europe.

Alaska, Canada / New England
For casual days at sea: jeans or slacks and a sweater with low-heeled shoes for deck activities.

For evenings, three types of attire will be appropriate: *Casual:* dresses or slacks and blouses for women; sport shirts and trousers for men

Smart casual: dresses or pantsuits for women; sport shirts, trousers and jackets for men

Formal: cocktail dresses for women; suits and ties, or tuxedos for men.

Alaska, Canada / New England

Women's Clothing Checklist

- ❑ jeans
- ❑ slacks
- ❑ sweaters
- ❑ dresses
- ❑ blouses
- ❑ pantsuits
- ❑ cocktail dress
- ❑ windbreaker
- ❑ jacket
- ❑ swimwear
- ❑ scarves/hat/cap
- ❑ low heeled walking shoes
- ❑ hiking boots/walking shoes
- ❑ dress shoes
- ❑ dancing shoes

Alaska, Canada / New England

Men's Clothing Checklist

- ❑ jeans
- ❑ slacks
- ❑ sports shirts

❏ sweaters
❏ trousers
❏ sport jackets
❏ suits and ties or tuxedos
❏ windbreaker
❏ jacket
❏ swimwear
❏ hat/cap
❏ low heeled walking shoes
❏ hiking boots/walking shoes
❏ dress shoes

Caribbean, Bahamas, Bermuda

For casual days onboard you'll be most comfortable in sports clothes and resort wear with low-heeled for deck activities. Bring several swimsuits!

Best bets on evening wear:

Casual: slacks and blouses or sundresses for women; sport shirts and trousers for men

Smart casual: pantsuits or dresses for women; jackets for men

Formal: cocktail dresses for women; suits and ties, or tuxedos for men.

Caribbean, Bahamas, Bermuda

Women's Clothing Checklist

❏ shirts
❏ shorts/skirts
❏ blouses
❏ slacks
❏ sundresses

- ❏ dresses
- ❏ pantsuits
- ❏ cocktail dress
- ❏ wrap or sweater (cool evenings)
- ❏ swimwear (several swimsuits!)
- ❏ sun hat/cap
- ❏ low heeled walking shoes
- ❏ sandals
- ❏ dress shoes
- ❏ dancing shoes

Caribbean, Bahamas, Bermuda

Men's Clothing Checklist

- ❏ shirts
- ❏ shorts
- ❏ jeans
- ❏ slacks
- ❏ sports shirts
- ❏ trousers
- ❏ sport jackets
- ❏ suits and ties or tuxedos
- ❏ swimwear
- ❏ hat/cap
- ❏ low heeled walking shoes
- ❏ sandals
- ❏ dress shoes

Mexico, Hawaii, Panama Canal

For casual days onboard you'll feel comfortable in sports clothes and resort wear with low-heeled shoes for deck activities. Bring several swimsuits.

Three types of appropriate evening wear:

Casual: sundresses or slacks and blouses for women; sport shirts and trousers for men.

Smart casual: dresses or pantsuits for women; jackets for men.

Formal: cocktail dresses for women; suits and ties, or tuxedos for men.

Mexico, Hawaii, Panama Canal

Women's Clothing Checklist
- ❑ shirts
- ❑ shorts/skirts
- ❑ blouses
- ❑ slacks
- ❑ sundresses
- ❑ dresses
- ❑ pantsuits
- ❑ cocktail dress
- ❑ wrap or sweater (cool evenings)
- ❑ swimwear (several swimsuits!)
- ❑ sun hat/cap
- ❑ low heeled walking shoes
- ❑ sandals
- ❑ dress shoes
- ❑ dancing shoes

Mexico, Hawaii, Panama Canal

Men's Clothing Checklist

- ❏ shirts
- ❏ shorts
- ❏ jeans
- ❏ slacks
- ❏ sports shirts
- ❏ trousers
- ❏ sport jackets
- ❏ suits and ties or tuxedos
- ❏ swimwear
- ❏ hat/cap
- ❏ low heeled walking shoes
- ❏ sandals
- ❏ dress shoes

Europe

For casual days onboard: sports clothes and resort wear with low-heeled shoes for deck activities. Best bets on evening wear:

Casual: dresses or slacks and blouses for women; sport shirts and trousers for men.

Smart casual: dresses or pantsuits for women; sports shirts, trousers and jackets for men.

Formal: cocktail dresses for women; suits and ties, or tuxedos for men.

Northern European nights can be cool, so bring sweaters, jackets and long pants. Pack a light raincoat, travel umbrella plus hiking boots or sturdy walking shoes for treks through cobblestone streets.

Europe

Women's Clothing Checklist

- ❏ shirts
- ❏ shorts/skirts
- ❏ blouses
- ❏ slacks
- ❏ sundresses
- ❏ dresses
- ❏ pantsuits
- ❏ cocktail dress
- ❏ wrap or sweater (cool evenings)
- ❏ swimwear
- ❏ scarves/hat/cap
- ❏ low heeled walking shoes
- ❏ hiking boots
- ❏ sandals
- ❏ dress shoes
- ❏ dancing shoes
- ❏ raincoat/travel umbrella

Europe

Men's Clothing Checklist

- ❏ shirts
- ❏ shorts
- ❏ jeans
- ❏ slacks
- ❏ sports shirts
- ❏ trousers
- ❏ sport jackets
- ❏ suits and ties or tuxedos
- ❏ swimwear
- ❏ hat/cap

- ❏ low heeled walking shoes
- ❏ hiking boots
- ❏ sandals
- ❏ dress shoes
- ❏ raincoat/travel umbrella

Disney Cruise Line tips on what to wear to dinner:

Casual restaurants: open-collar shirts and slacks for men and pants and a blouse or a casual dress for ladies. Formal restaurants: jacket for men and dresses or pantsuits for ladies. Like most major cruise lines, Disney Cruise Line requests that no shorts, T-shirts, or jeans be worn in any of the restaurants in the evening.

Windjammer Barefoot Cruises takes another tack...

Kick off your shoes and get ready for an adventure you'll never forget. Informality rules! T-shirts and shorts are all you need.

What to pack for your Windjammer cruise:

Swim Suits • T-shirts • Shorts • Beach Towel • Tennis/Walking Shoes • Personal Toiletries • Camera & Film • Sunglasses • Hat • Sun Screen • Mini Binoculars • Long Pants • Sun Dress• Fun Items •

Tag Your Bags

Tag your bags: Write your name, sailing date and stateroom number clearly on the paper tags provided by the cruise line. Attach a second sturdy luggage tag with your name address, home telephone number.

Resources: books
Fodor's *How to Pack: Experts Share Tips and Techniques to Make Packing a Breeze*, Cardone, Laurel.

Packing Bags to Trunks, Gross, Kim Johnson

The Packing Book: Secrets of the Carry-on Traveler, Gilford

Pack It Up: A Book for the Contemporary Traveler, McAlpin, Anne

F. Special Interest/Theme Cruises

From archaeology to auto-racing, chances are there's a theme cruise or special guest programming about your favorite hobby. Celebrities, best-selling authors, sports stars and specialists - they're all aboard for your entertainment.

Here's an example of theme cruises and seminar topics offered by special guests.

NCL's theme cruises feature an on-board program of exciting events for people with a special interest in music or sports. Meet 'Hall of Famers,' hear the legends of Jazz and Blues, or play on the world's finest courses with the year-round Tee-Up Cruises®. NCL now offers Sports Illustrated Afloat™ theme cruise.

Five of today's hottest trends have inspired theme cruises on select worldwide itineraries aboard the **Crystal Cruises** fleet.

'Celebration of Swing' offers big band music and swing dancing; 'Wine & Food Festival' presents the art of gourmet wine and food pairing; 'Health and Fitness' features workshops and tips for leading healthier, more rewarding lives; 'Best of Broadway' celebrates legendary talents in the arts and entertainment world and 'Computer University @ Sea' explores electronic advances and personal computer skills.

Silversea Cruises' exclusive Le Cordon Bleu Culinary Cruise Series introduces guests to the finer points of l'art culinaire from Master Chefs of the Le Cordon Bleu Academy. The program includes lectures, cooking demonstrations and wine tastings hosted by the Le Cordon Bleu Master Chefs. Guests aboard these Epicurean adventures can compete against fellow passengers in cooking competitions and "go to market" with the chefs while in Bali and Casablanca.

Highlights of Theme and Special Interest Programming

Fitness at Sea

Most ships are sporting the latest workout equipment as more space onboard is dedicated to fitness. Celebrity Cruises AquaSpa makes working out more fun with virtual reality stationary bicycles. Holland America Line 'Passport to Fitness Program' offers seminars on such topics as back care, foot care, de-stressing & aromatherapy, fitness & nutrition.

ICE SKATING!! Royal Caribbean's Voyager of the Seas is the first cruise ship in history to offer passengers the exhilarating experience of ice skating on the high seas.

Artistically inclined? Cruises invite a variety of artists aboard for workshops and seminars. Examples: Cartoon 'Hall of Famer' Mike Peters, creator of Mother Goose and Grimm. "Grimmy" is syndicated to more than 800 newspapers in all 50 US states and 12 other countries. Mike has spoken on such topics as "The Wacky World of Cartooning," and "The Art of Caricature."

For Baseball Fans

Pinch hit with some of baseball's most renowned, aboard the annual NCL Pro Baseball Cruise. Ask your favorite pros questions and get their autographs!

For Computer Buffs

NCL's M/S Norwegian Sky hosts the Internet Cafe for guests wishing to go online at sea. Located within the ship's coffee bar, the Internet Cafe is equipped with nine computer terminals, available 24 hours-a-day. Guests can send and receive e-mail, check the stock market and more. The Norwegian Sky is also the first NCL ship to offer in-stateroom connections to the Internet.

Internet Cafe or in-stateroom usage is $19.95 per hour or 33 cents per minute. Too pricey for casual surfing, perhaps, but a true bargain for communicating with friends, family and business associates ashore. NCL also plans to offer laptop computer rentals aboard the Sky. Next online in NCL's fleet? The S/S Norway.

Computer geeks unite! Geek Cruises, Caribbean voyages for geeks and hacks May 2000, January 2001 [http://www.GeekCruises.com]]

Military Veterans

Cruises are a favorite of veterans who want to revisit favorite places from their tours of duty. Reunions aboard a cruise provide a great atmosphere for sharing war stories and catching up with old friends. Vets spouse and families will enjoy the vacation as well.

Contact Galaxy Tours, Box 234, Wayne, Pennsylvania 19087 (800) 523-7287 or Valor Tours, Ltd.

10 Liberty Ship Way, #160, Sausalito, California 94965 (415) 332-7850, (800) 842-4504

Go Natural! Cruises for Nudists

Bring sunscreen and a smile! Contact the American Association for Nude Recreation, 1703 N. Main Street, Suite E, Kissimmee, FL 34744-3396, (800) TRY-NUDE or (407) 933-2064.

Golf!

Whether you're a scratch golfer, a duffer or a "weekend warrior," Carnival Cruise Lines offers golfers of any proficiency level an opportunity to play top courses in the Bahamas, Mexico and the Caribbean, as well as receive one-on-one instruction from teaching professionals.

Lessons are provided both aboard ship and during golf excursions by golf professionals, who combine their years of teaching experience with state-of-the-art computer technology to help golfers improve their game.

Shipboard lessons are available in 30- or 60-minute increments and take place in a netted "driving range" where golfers' swings are videotaped and then analyzed via computer by the professional on board. A take-home video recap, complete with step-by-step voice-over instruction and stop-action/ slow-motion analysis, is provided with each lesson.

Included in port-of-call excursion packages are green fees, professional instruction, cart rental or caddie, and transportation to and from shoreside courses. Equipment rental, including top-of-the-line Callaway clubs, is also available. A wide variety of golfing accessories such as golf balls, gloves, tees, etc., are available for purchase, as well.

More than a dozen different golf courses are featured within the program, including The Links at Safe Haven in Grand Cayman, The Key West Golf Club, the southernmost golf course in the US; and St. Thomas' Mahogany Run.

Carnival's golf program is available onboard all ships except Tropicale. Prices begin at $40 for shipboard lessons and $100 for shoreside golf excursions, which include on-site instruction from golf professionals.

See the *Cruise Guide to Activities* for special interest cruises and the *Best of the Best Awards* at our Web site **www.cruisechooser.com**.

G. Documents

Passports and other important documents.

Which documents do I need in order to cruise?
•What information do I need to get a new passport

or renew an expired passport? • Where do I get my passport? • Where should I carry important documents? • Where should I keep them while onboard?

Which documents do I need in order to cruise?

Everyone needs ID. You will not be allowed to board the ship without proper ID. Every member of your party is required to have ID, including infants and children.

Where can I find more about needed documents?

1. Carefully read the last pages of your cruise brochure.

2. Ask your travel agent.

3. Online: go to the US State Department [http://travel.state.gov]   or British Foreign Office: [http://www.fco.gov.uk/travel/]

4. Telephone: Office of Passport Services (202) 647-0518 or US State Department: (202) 647-5225

Document requirements vary depending on:

1. your citizenship

2. port of departure

3. itinerary

4. length of stay

Citizenship & Documents

• US citizen but no passport? You must bring a photo ID and proof of citizenship: voter ID card or birth certificate or a certified copy. A driver's license is not enough.

- Non-US citizen but a US resident departing from the US? You must bring your alien- registration card and passport.
- Non-US citizen departing from a US port? Bring your passport and visa, (if required).

Cruise Chooser Passport Checklist

What information do I need to get a new passport or renew an expired passport?

1. Proof of citizenship: birth certificate or a certified copy. Contact your local Health Department about cost and documentation needed to obtain a certified copy of your birth certificate.

2. A driver's license (or other photo ID with your signature.)

3. The old passport.

4. Two identical recent 2X2 inch photos with a full view of your face.

5. Documents showing any name change.

Two options for getting a passport.

1. Go in person to a passport agency. United States Passport agencies are located in Boston, Chicago, Honolulu, Houston, Los Angeles, Miami, New Orleans, New York City, Philadelphia, San Francisco, Seattle, Stamford, Conn. and Washington , DC.

Bring with you: all of the above documents, ID's and photos.

2. If you don't live near a passport agency city, (Check the US Government listings in the phone book before you go.) Ask to have your passport sent to a passport agency by overnight or priority delivery

and send SASE (self addressed stamped envelope) with postage for overnight or priority return delivery.

Where should I carry important documents? Where should I keep them while onboard?

Keep your passport, ID and other documents along with cash, and credit cards on your person in a travel wallet or belly bag or in a secure carry-on bag or purse. Do not be careless with your ID. Once onboard, you can store your documents in your stateroom safe or the ship's safe, until needed.

Attention Century Club Members!

An Official Port of Entry Stamp from foreign countries you've visited may well become one of your most treasured travel souvenirs. Especially if you're 'adding up countries' to join the Century Club (Travel to 100 countries is the minimum membership requirement.)

H. Insurance

Do I need travel insurance/trip cancellation insurance?

Trip cancellation insurance is a worthwhile investment, with its biggest payoff being your peace of mind. If an accident, illness or family emergency prevents you from taking your cruise, you'll recover your ticket price.

Trip cancellation insurance is available through the cruise line, your travel agent and most credit cards offer travel accident and emergency assistance insurance.

Sample Travel Insurance

Travelex Insurance Services
[http://www.travelex-insurance.com]
(800) 228-9792

Travel Guard
[http://www.thetravelsite.com/insurance.html]
Call Toll Free (888) 826-1300

Travel Insurance Services
[http://www.travelinsure.com/]
(800) 937-1387 or (925) 932-1387 (California, USA)
Brochures via Fax-on-Demand: (24 hours)
(800) 937-1387, extension 500.

Worldwide Travel Insurance Limited
[http://www.wwtis.co.uk/]
England Tel : +44 (0)1892 833338 Fax: +44 (0)1892 837744 01892

Travel and Emergency Assistance VISA Gold
Call the Visa Assistance Center (800) VISA-911,
(800) 847-2911).
Services include: emergency message service, medical referral assistance, legal referral assistance, emergency transportation assistance, emergency ticket replacement, lost luggage locator service,

emergency translation service, prescription assistance and valuable document delivery arrangements, pre-trip assistance, emergency cash, emergency card replacement.

VISA Gold's Pre-Trip Assistance Service can give you information on your destination before you leave - such as ATM locations, currency exchange rates, weather reports, health precautions, immunizations and required visas.

Clipper Cruise Line offers automatic $250,000 Travel Insurance Policy subject to policy terms and limitations.

Royal Caribbean International offers a CruiseCare Passenger Protection Plan, which reimburses up to the full value of your cruise. The CruiseCare Plan also offers affordable medical, travel, baggage and personal injury coverage for the duration of your cruise. Consult your travel agent about other cruise line offers.

Medical Air ambulance system MEDJET [http://www.medjetassistance.com] Annual fee is $150 for individuals and $225 for a family of up to five children. Members who become hospitalized 150 miles or more from home will be flown to their hometown hospital on a private Lear jet equipped as a hospital intensive-care unit. A physician and nurse will accompany you onboard. Call 800-9-MEDJET.

Cruise Line Bonding Insurance
& Financial Responsibility

Throughout the last 25 years of cruise industry growth, passengers sailing on ships serving US ports have been protected by a performance bond administered by the Federal Maritime Commission (FMC). The bond covers passenger refunds for "non-performance of transportation."

I. Health Tips

How Can I Prevent Jet Lag? Seasickness? What kind of medical care will I find onboard? Will I need immunizations/vaccinations? How can I use ship sanitation scores?

Preventing Jet Lag

You cross the gangway and leave that workaday world behind. Can't wait to start your vacation? You may want to factor in some 'down time' that first day for your body to adjust to new time zones, new surroundings and the excitement (stress) your body has experienced en route.

Here are several practical methods that will help you avoid jet lag and squeeze the most fun out of every vacation minute.

Adjust your body's 'clock.'

You can prepare your body to adjust to the stress of hopping time zones by changing its circadian rhythm. Adjust your body's clock by changing your

150

routine bedtime, morning awakening and meal times. Begin one week in advance of your trip. Going eastward? Get up an hour earlier and eat one hour earlier each day Heading westward? Add an hour to your wake-up and meal times

High energy tips:
   While traveling to the port, eat light food, avoid carbonated beverages, avoid caffeine (tea, coffee, cola, chocolate, some over-the-counter medicines.) Drink more water (bring a non-carbonated bottle of water with you.) Take exercise breaks - for stretching or yoga breathing.

   Resources: The Argonne Anti-Jet Lag Diet, Argonne National Laboratories, 97 South Class Avenue, Argonne, IL 60439.   (708) 252- 5575
   Free: Defeating Jet Lag, Forsyth Travel Library, 9154 West 57th St., Box 2975, Shawnee Mission, KS 66201. Send SASE (business sized envelope)

Preventing Seasickness
   Is it the tip of the ship or the motion of the ocean?

Choose the right vessel.
   Cruise ships have come a long way in stability and comfort. Underwater wing-like stabilizers that reduce pitch and roll are common on most ships built in the last 20 years. Stable ship styles for unstable stomachs: Transatlantic liners with deep drafts,

Catamaran (divided dual hull) such as the Radisson Diamond, Sailing ships such as Clipper, Windstar.

Choose the right itinerary.

No sea legs? Sail the sheltered waters and rivers until you're more at ease. Landlubbers will have no qualms with Alaska's Inside Passage; US & European river cruises; winter, spring, summer in the lovely Gulf of Mexico, Eastern and Western Caribbean; and summer in the Mediterranean.

Wanna' rough it? Be our guest and sail the fast currents of South Africa's Cape of Good Hope or South America's Cape Horn. You can also count on some swells in the North Atlantic and the South China Sea.

Easy prevention and remedies:

Non-prescription medicine

Antihistamines such as Bonine or Dramamine can be taken before you even step aboard, but often cause drowsiness. Dramamine is also available by injection. Please consult your doctor.

Herbal aids

Ginger root capsules and teas. Long popular with expectant mothers, ginger is nature's affordable and virtually side-effect free calmative.

Accupressure

Travel Garde or Sea Band knit wrist bands press pea-size nodes into accupressure points to relieve symptoms of nausea.

Diet

Avoid having a empty stomach (not too difficult on most cruises.) Try Mom's recipe of dry bread, toast, crackers and a carbonated caffeine-free beverage such as ginger ale or seltzer water. Avoid overeating and greasy or spicy foods.

Action

Take a walk in the fresh air - and focus on the horizon

Health Tips for Families

"Before I travel with the children," says Janet Harris, "I always put together an Emergency Medical Checklist. Its an expanded vacation-version of what I post on the refrigerator for baby-sitters. In addition to emergency phone numbers for their pediatrician and grandparents, I list any medications, allergies or special diets and any other special needs."

An Ounce of Prevention

Be sure to pack children's aspirin and cold medications, prescriptions, sunscreen, insect repellent, band aids and a child's thermometer. When you tour the ship, locate the ship's medical office.

Consult with your travel agent and pediatrician when you book your cruise- and schedule immunizations at least 30 days before your departure date.

Immunization/Vaccination information online:
International Society of Travel Medicine
[http://www.istm.com]
International Travel and Health (World Health organization) [http:// www.who.ch]
Center for Disease Control Travel Information CDC [http://www.cdc.gov/travel/index.html]
Travel Health Online
[http://www.tripprep.com/index]

Smoke-free
Serious non-smokers have found paradise, Carnival Cruise Line's Paradise, that is. Occupancy levels aboard the world's first smoke-free ship are averaging 112 percent.

"While many in the industry questioned the wisdom of launching a totally smoke-free ship, these figures confirm there is a strong consumer demand for this unique smoke-free vacation option," says Bob Dickinson, President, Carnival Cruise Lines.

Not everyone aboard Paradise has lived up to the promise of seven days of smoke-free Caribbean cruising, however. At least nine passengers -- each of whom signed documents pledging not to smoke on board -- have been asked to disembark the vessel, forfeit their cruise fare and return home at their own expense.

Health Care Guidelines for Cruise Ship Medical Facilities.

Medical infirmaries and personnel vary from ship-to-ship based on a variety of factors including the size of the vessel, the number of passengers and crew, and the length and itinerary of the cruise.

In 1995, the ICCL formed a working group of medical experts to examine the issue of shipboard medical facilities, which produced the 1996 released Medical Facilities Guidelines. These guidelines reflect the recommendations of this group as they relate to the facilities, staffing, equipment and procedures for medical infirmaries on cruise ships. They were developed with the input of the ACEP and were revised and updated in both 1997 and 1998.

The guidelines are designed to foster the goal of providing reasonable emergency medical care for passengers and crew aboard cruise vessels. Patients requiring more comprehensive facilities are typically referred for treatment to a shoreside facility.

The American College of Emergency Physicians, ACEP, believes that appropriate emergency care and health care maintenance for passengers and crew members aboard ships sailing in international waters are desirable. The cruise ship industry and its medical departments should retain medical personnel who can:

• Provide quality maritime medical care for passengers and crew members aboard cruise ships

• Initiate appropriate stabilization, diagnostic, and therapeutic maneuvers for critically ill or medically unstable patients

• Support, comfort, and care for patients on board ship

• Assist, in conjunction with the cruise line, in the medical evacuation of patients in a timely fashion when appropriate.

Prior to booking a cruise, passengers should assess individual health requirements and consider those requirements when deciding on a cruise vacation. In all cases, potential passengers with a serious medical condition should consult with their personal physician prior to taking any vacation.

Good care is within reach.

Princess Cruises has equipped its entire fleet with more than 65 automatic external defibrillators (AEDs) to assist in the treatment of sudden cardiac arrest. The portable defibrillators, which augment larger defibrillators currently found in all Princess shipboard medical centers, will provide the quickest possible care in the event of a cardiac emergency while at sea. The portable and lightweight Heartstream

ForeRunner AED is more accessible for immediate use by emergency medical technicians, doctors, nurses, security personnel.

Princess Cruises also offers a new telemedicine technology which gives the ship's doctors worldwide access to specialist medical support. MedServe Axcess uses a combination of satellite and Internet technology, to transmit digitized x-ray images and other medical data to on-call consultants who can then provide specialist medical advice within minutes.

"All our shipboard medical centers operate with a full line of equipment and supplies, as typically found in a small hospital emergency room, said Dr. Alastair Smith, Princess' vice president of fleet medical. Each center is also staffed by a full-time team of experienced British-registered doctors and nurses.

Health-conscious vacationers will appreciate Carnival Cruise Lines' Nautica Spa Fare, delicious guilt-free dishes available on all menus. These are designated by a special symbol as lower in fat, cholesterol, sodium and calories. Meats, fish and poultry are broiled or roasted, salads are prepared with low-fat free dressings and desserts with sugar substitutes.

Ship's Sanitation Scores

The Centers for Disease Control and Prevention (CDC), a division of the US Public Health Service, regulates sanitary conditions on all foreign-flag passenger vessels visiting US ports. (US flagged ships are under the jurisdiction of the Food & Drug Administration.) Most infractions involve improper food handling, and temperature violations in food preparation, holding and serving areas.

Unannounced inspections are carried out at regular intervals, but if a ship fails, it can remedy the problem and request a reinspection. The CDC can recommend that a ship not sail due to sanitation violations, but cooperation is voluntary.

How to use the sanitation scores:
Your best bet is to look for trends over time, with a passing grade of at least 86 out of a possible 100. You can often find recent scores in your local newspaper's Sunday Travel section. Scores are available online at [http://www.cdc.gov//pub/ship_inspections/shipscore.txt] or call (404) 332-4565. Ask for document 510051.

Will you need a vacation after your vacation?

On your next cruise, get the most rest from your "down" time, with short catnaps and plan a minimum number of hours into your schedule for a good night's sleep. For tips on preserving that go-go-go

high energy while on vacation, check out Power
Sleep by Dr. James Maas, professor, sleep expert and
past chair of Cornell University's psychology department. FREEBIE: Order a free copy of Dr. Mass' free
brochure "Wake-Up Call: A guide to a Good Night's
Sleep," call toll-free (877) 4U2-REST.

J. **Personal Safety & Security Tips**

What security measures do cruise lines follow?
What are the latest safety regulations for ships? What
about rough weather?

Safety & Security Aboard
All cruise ships are subject to strict international
standards and regulations set forth by the
International Maritime Organization (IMO), an arm of
the United Nations. As an IMO member, the US
actively supports the development of these standards
and is responsible for oversight of all ships calling on
US ports. You can view the results of US Coast Guard
quarterly inspections at [http://www.imo.org]. The
passenger cruise industry is also regulated by eight
other US government agencies.

In the last decade, *more than 44 million people*
sailed from US ports without a single passenger death
due to a marine incident on an ICCL member cruise
line vessel.

A cruise ship is inherently secure because it is a controlled environment with limited access. In order to maintain this secure environment, cruise lines have established strict and highly confidential ship security procedures which are based partly on internationally agreed-upon measures set forth by the International Maritime Organization (IMO).

The security initiatives, referred to as IMO Measures To Prevent Unlawful Acts Against Passengers and Crews on Board Ships, were adopted in 1986 and outline specific procedures that cruise ships, ports and flag states must follow in regard to security.

Security Overview - IMO Measures
• ship operators are required to restrict access to authorized personnel
• ship operators are required to monitor the flow of materials brought on board a ship in port.
• At US cruise terminals, port security mirrors airport procedures such as inspection of all carry-on baggage and the use of metal detectors.

The US Coast Guard implemented an Interim Final Rule on Security for Passenger Vessels and Passenger Terminals which adopted these IMO measures effective 1996. This rule sets three levels of security (low, medium and high) based on the nature of the threat received.

The regulations require operators to submit a

comprehensive Vessel Security Plan to the US Coast Guard for each passenger vessel and port terminal which outlines security procedures for screening of passengers, baggage and ship supplies, as well as limits access to the vessel and terminal facility.

All ICCL member lines have submitted security plans which have been accepted by the Coast Guard; and are reviewed annually.

The cruise industry works with federal, state, and local agencies that have jurisdiction over security matters.

What's being done:

• The International Council of Cruise Lines, ICCL is a member of a US Interagency Task Force on Passenger Vessel Security which establishes procedures and updates security measures designed to maintain security at US ports of embarkation.

• Cruise lines employ security experts and advisors and train onboard personnel in security procedures.

• The Department of State and the US Coast Guard have established industry training programs that address seaport security.

• The Coast Guard conducts annual port vulnerability-risk assessment studies at US ports.

Source: International Council of Cruise Lines, ICCL. With special thanks to Bridget Ann Serchak.

Safety of Life at Sea SOLAS

Shape up or ship out! Rigorous SOLAS regulations implemented in 1997 apply to all ships calling on US ports. The US Coast Guard makes and initial inspection of new ships and ships making their first call to a US port, followed by quarterly inspections.

The Coast Guard examines the vessel from stem to stern, carefully assessing machinery and structural soundness from the engine room to the bridge. Ship's staff & crew run through lifesaving procedures including fire safety and use of emergency equipment. SOLAS required older vessels to be refurbished and remodeled with sprinkler systems, low-level lighting systems and freon-free air-conditioning systems.

Vessels which required too many costly modifications to make the cut no longer call on US ports. Beware the bargain that's too good to be true. Non-SOLAS certified vessels are in operation in the Mediterranean and Asian marketplace.

Seven Short and One Long
(The Lifeboat Drill)

Seven short and one long blast of the ship's whistle is the emergency signal to "muster" or gather at your lifeboat station. All passengers and crew are required to join in a mandatory lifeboat drill within 24 hours after sailing from the port of embarkation. Here's what to expect:

Lifeboat Drill Checklist

✔ Return immediately to your stateroom to get your life jacket. No need to put the life jacket on yet. A crew member will assist you at your 'muster' (gathering) station.

✔ Leave all other items, luggage, purses, camera equipment and pool gear in your stateroom.
✔ Bring your room key.
✔ Smoking and drinking during the drill is prohibited.
✔ Follow the directions on the back of your stateroom door or wall to your lifeboat station.
✔ Follow the directions of your steward and other crew members.
✔ Take the stairs to your muster station - since elevators will likely be off limits in an actual emergency.

This mandatory drill may well be the only serious event during your cruise - please be respectful of directions on the public address system and the instructions of crew members.

Smoke on the Water?
Princess Cruises ships are now equipped with Emergency Escape Smoke Hoods. The EVAC-U8 is a state-of the-art respiratory protection device that provides up to 20 minutes of breathable air in a toxic environment. Princess is deploying between 350 and 700 units per vessel for use by crew members.

Weather & Storms

"Everybody talks about the weather but nobody does anything about it." Mark Twain.

Considering cruising the Caribbean during Hurricane Season? Look into itineraries with southern islands outside the primary "hurricane belt." *Outside the belt*: Aruba, Bonaire, Curacao, the Venezuelan coast. Visit the Caribbean Tourism Organization, CTO Web site [http://www.caritourism.com].

Cruise companies are well prepared to deal with any challenges brought on by stormy weather. The safety of the passenger and crew come first. One advantage of traveling by ship? Unlike land-based vacations, cruise ships can change course to avoid dangerous weather. Cruise lines will change itineraries, embarkation and departure times, and usually fly passengers home from the closest port if a cruise is canceled. Most cruise line headquarters have emergency preparedness plans to insure 'business as usual.' Royal Caribbean International's additional operations center in Colorado will be all-systems-go despite any stormy weather at their Miami headquarters.

Safety & Security Ashore

The US State Department and the British Foreign Office are the best sources for up-to-date health and safety information on your destination.
resources: US State Department: (202) 647-5225, [http://travel.state.gov/] (click on "travel warnings" for an alphabetized list.) British Foreign Office: [http://www.fco.gov.uk/travel/countryadvice.asp].

Pay attention to 'public announcements,' issued

whenever terrorist threats or other conditions pose a significant though short-term risk to the security of US travelers. The US State Department's advisories identify 'volatile and unpredictable' political climates and even 'geological' threats such as volcanic eruptions in Ecuador or Montserrat.

You thought your town had crazy drivers...

Turkey's notorious erratic drivers spurred US State Department officials to warn unfamiliar visitors to "avoid driving at night."

Brazilian government officials recommend running red lights between 10 p.m. and 6 a.m., due to recent car jackings.

Pass Go and collect $200

Travelers who find themselves in trouble, may discover that working with US authorities can be a complicated affair. US consulates exist within range of most ports-of-call, but don't expect instant access simply because you're a 'Taxpaying American Citizen.' Many countries have been known to delay assistance for those arrested for suspected terrorist, or drug-related activities. Don't fall prey to smuggler's easy money schemes such as a request for you, the innocent tourist to "take this package back to my aunt in Miami." Follow the rules (even if you are on vacation!)

PART 5
Trends in Cruising

A. **Growth & Expansion:**
- ◆ New Ships "Newbuilds" through 2005
- ◆ "One-Upsman-Ship" What's New
  With the Newest Ships.

B. **Accommodations**
- ◆ New Stateroom Extras.
- ◆ Fun Public Areas: casinos, lounges, spas, pools.
- ◆ High Technology on the High Seas.

C. **Activities**
- ◆ Entertainment!

D. **Dining** - What's New.

E. **Destinations**
- ◆ Shore Excursions especially for you.
- ◆ Ports of Departure.
- ◆ Cruising and the Environment.

A. **Trends in Growth and Expansion**

Cruising's Future is Full Speed Ahead! New Ships
'Newbuilds' through 2005

> *"If it works, we'll grow it. We're going for the gold,"*
> Michael Eisner, Chairman, Walt Disney Co.,
> commenting on Disney Cruise Line's debut.

The Cruise Industry is Booming

With 55 newbuilds on order through 2005, cruise
fans have a lot to look forward to: new ships, exotic
itineraries and super savings. Cruise companies will
have 43 percent more beds to fill; more than double
the increase over the previous five-year period; giving
value shoppers plenty of bargains to choose from.
Executives and investors are betting that demand will
soon catch up with supply, since passenger boardings
increased by 73 percent between 1995 - 2000.

Multi-Million Dollar Investments
Highlights

$7 billion is Carnival Corporation's total estimated
value for new ships scheduled for delivery in the next
five years. Including Cunard's Queen Mary 2, Carnival
Corporation currently has 16 new vessels on order;
seven ships for Carnival (Spirit, Pride, Conquest, Glory,
Legend, Valor and Miracle), five unnamed vessels for
Holland America Line and three unnamed Costa ships.

Norwegian Cruise Line has ordered two new Sky-class vessels with pre-construction prices of $351 million and $334 million.

Star Cruises has four newbuilds on order with an estimated value of $1.8 billion.

$5.6 billion is Royal Caribbean International's estimated value for 10 new ships; three Celebrity Cruises vessels (Infinity, Summit and unnamed), three more Voyager-class vessels (Adventure of the Seas and two unnamed) and four Vantage-class ships (Radianceof the Seas, Brilliance of the Seas and two unnamed.)

Princess Cruises has six new ships on order (Golden Princess, Star Princess, Coral Princess, Island Princess, Diamond Princess and Sapphire Princess.) These new vessels have an estimated pricetag of 2.2 billion.

All amounts are in US dollars.

55 NEWBUILDS TO LAUNCH 2001-2005!

Cruise Line	Name	Capacity

2001
*TBA = to be announced

Cruise Line	Name	Capacity
Carnival Cruise Lines	Carnival Spirit	2,112
Carnival Cruise Lines	Carnival Pride	2,112
Celebrity Cruises	Celebrity Summit	1,950
Celebrity Cruises	Celebrity Infinity	1,950
Delta Queen Coastal Cruises	Cape May Light	226
Delta QueenCoastal Cruises	Cape Cod Light	226
Festival Cruises/First European Cruises	European Vision	1,250
Norwegian Cruise Line	Norwegian Sun	2,000
Princess Cruises	Golden Princess	2,600
Radisson Seven Seas Cruises	Seven Seas Mariner	360
Renaissance Cruise	R8	684
Royal Caribbean Intl.	Radiance of the Seas	2,000
Royal Caribbean Intl.	Adventure of the Seas	3,100
Royal Olympic Cruises	Olympic Explorer	840
Silversea Cruises	Silver Whisper	396
Star Cruises	SuperStar Libra	TBA

2002

Cruise Line	Name	Capacity
Carnival Cruise Lines	Conquest	2,758
Carnival Cruise Lines	Legend	2,112
Celebrity Cruises	TBA Millennium-class	1,950
Festival Cruises/First European Cruises	European Dream	1,250
Holland America Line	New class	TBA
Norwegian Cruise Line	Sky-class vessel	2,000
Norwegian Cruise Line	SuperStar Libra-class vessel	TBA
Princess Cruises	Star Princess	2,600
Princess Cruises	Coral Princess	1,950

ResidenSea . . . . .World of ResidenSea 285
Royal Caribbean Intl. . . . . .Brilliance of the Seas 2,000
Royal Caribbean Intl. . . . . .Voyager-class 3,100
Star Cruises . . . . .SuperStar Scorpio 400

2003

American Classic Voyages Co. . . . . .Project America #1 1,900
Carnival Cruise Lines . . . . .Glory .2,758
Carnival Cruise Lines . . . . .Miracle 2,758
Costa Cruises .TBA .TBA
Costa Cruises .TBA .TBA
Crystal Cruises . . . . .TBA .TBA
Cunard . . . . .Queen Mary II 2,500
Holland America Line . . . . .New class . . . . .TBA
Holland America Line . . . . .New class . . . . .TBA
Royal Caribbean International . . . . . . .Vantage-class 2,000
Royal Caribbean Intl. . . . . .Voyager-class 3,100
Star Cruises . . . . .SuperStar Sagittarius II 3,000
United States Lines . . . . .TBA .TBA

2004

American Classic Voyages Co. . . . . .Project America #2 1,900
Carnival Cruise Lines . . . . .Valor .2,758
Holland America Line . . . . .New class . . . . .TBA
P & O . . . . .unnamed . . . . .TBA
Princess Cruises . . . . .Island Princess 2,600
Royal Caribbean International . . . . . . .Vantage-Class 2,000
United States Lines . . . . .TBA .TBA

2005

World City	America World City	6,200
Star Cruises	SuperStar Capricorn II	3,000
Holland America Line	New class	TBA
Holland America Line	New class	TBA

2003-2005

Costa Cruises	TBA	TBA
Princess Cruises	Diamond Princess	1,950
Princess Cruises	Sapphire Princess	2,600

55 NEW SHIPS ON ORDER THROUGH 2005 (by Cruise Line)

Cruise Line	Ship Name	Year Due
American Classic Voyages Co.	Project America #1	2003
	Project America #2	2004
Carnival Cruise Line	Carnival Spirit	2001
	Carnival Pride	2001
	Conquest	2002
	Glory	2003
	Legend	2002
	Miracle	2003
	Valor	2004
Celebrity Cruises	Celebrity Infinity	2001
	Celebrity Summit	2001
	Millennium-class	2002

Costa Cruise Lines	TBA .2003
	TBA .2003
	TBA .2003-2005

| **Crystal Cruises** | TBA .2003 |

| **Cunard** | Queen Mary II . . . . .2003 |

| **Delta Queen Coastal Cruises** | Cape May Light . . . . .2001 |
| | Cape Cod Light . . . . .2001 |

Festival Cruises/First European Cruises

	European Vision 2001
	European Dream 2002
	Mistral-class 2003-2005
	Mistral-class 2003-2005

Holland America Line	New Class 2003
	New Class 2003
	New Class 2004
	New Class 2005
	New Class 2005

Norwegian Cruise Line	Norwegian Sun 2001
	Norwegian Sky-class vessel 2002
	SuperStar Libra-class . . . . .TBA

| **P & O** | Unnamed . . . . .2004 |

Princess Cruises	Golden Princess 2001
	Star Princess 2002
	Coral Princess 2002
	Island Princess 2004

Princess Cruises (continued)	Diamond Princess 2003-2005
	Sapphire Princess 2003-2005
Radisson Seven Seas Cruises	Seven Seas Mariner 2001
Renaissance Cruise	R8 .2001
ResidenSea Ltd.	The World of ResidenSea 2001
Royal Caribbean International	Radiance of the Seas 2001
	Adventure of the Seas 2001
	Brilliance of the Seas 2002
	Voyager-class vessel 2002
	Voyager-class vessel 2003
	Vantage-class vessel 2003
	Vantage-class vessel 2004
Royal Olympic Cruises	Olympic Explorer 2001
Silversea Cruises	Silver Whisper 2001
Star Cruises	SuperStar Libra 2001
	SuperStar Scorpio 2002
	SuperStar Sagittarius II 2003
	SuperStar Capricorn II 2005
United States Lines	TBA 2003
	TBA 2004
World City	America World City 2005

Tips for the Maiden Voyage/Shakedown Cruise

- Book with an experienced travel agent who will protect your interests in case of construction delays.

- Purchase an air/sea package - buy your airfare via the cruise line - you won't miss the boat.

- If you are celebrating a once-in-a-lifetime event that is date-critical, consider being more flexible with your embarkation date, or book on an existing ship.

- The first few voyages may not be perfect - food, service and entertainment are being fine-tuned.

- One thing you can be sure of, the best employees promote upwards to the newest ship, it's an honor and a reward. Service should be top-notch on a newbuild.

- Be dazzled! Cruise lines pull out all the stops to celebrate a maiden voyage!

What about possible construction delays?

With 55 ships on order from 2000 through 2005, and a limited number of cruise vessel shipyards; turnarounds are tight and some delivery deadlines are being pushed back. If your sailing is canceled due to construction delays, the cruise line will usually offer you another sailing date or transfer your reservation to another ship. Passengers who reschedule their voyage may receive compensation such as a 15- to 25 percent discount or shipboard credits up to

$200 per person. Many lines will issue a full refund and a future cruise credit of 10 percent or more, should you decide to cancel.

New Ship / New Currency
The Euro has been accepted as the official onboard currency of Festival Cruises' flagship Mistral. In the US, Festival is marketed as First European Cruises.

Virtual Reality Tours
Visit these sites for a virtual tour of these ships.

Royal Caribbean International's Voyager of the Seas
[http://www.rccl.com/voyageroftheseas/]

Holland America Line's Veendam
[http://www.hollandamerica.com/
vr/veendam_vr_index.html]

Princess Cruises' Grand Princess
[http://www.princesscruises.com/fleet/
grand/index.html]

Visit this site to view a video.
Radisson Seven Seas Navigator
[http://www.streamingtravel.com/]

176

Highlights of the Cruise Lines International Association's (CLIA)
Cruise Industry General Overview

The cruise industry is the fastest growing segment of the travel industry and has achieved more than 1,000 percent growth since 1970, when an estimated 500,000 people took a cruise. In 1998, 5.4 million people took a cruise. By 2000, CLIA estimates that as many as 7 million people will cruise each year.

The North American cruise industry's growth is also reflected by a big jump in capacity. During the 1980's some 40 new ships were built. Global capacity has also increased by almost 50 percent.

55 new vessels are on order for delivery by 2005.

Over the past six years, cruise vessel embarkations from North American ports have increased by almost 50 percent. 3 million plus passengers sailed from the Floridian ports of Miami, Port Everglades, Port Canaveral, and Port Tampa. A significant number of passengers also embarked from ports in Alaska, California, Louisiana, New York, Texas and Massachusetts.

3.5 million passengers boarded cruise vessels from ports outside North America.

Number of North American Passenger
Boardings: 5.5 million
Number of Total Worldwide Passenger
Boardings: 9.0 million
Number of Vessels Embarking from North
America: 131

The top cruise destination markets are the
Caribbean, Alaska, Mediterranean, Europe,
Trans-Canal (Panama), Mexico, and Bermuda.

source:
Cruise Lines International Association, CLIA
[http://www.cruising.org]

Made In the USA?

US law prohibits any ship not built in the US from flying a US flag. If your ship flies a Liberian or Panamanian flag, it's one of the majority: 80 percent of vessels calling on US ports are foreign-flagged. In the past 20 years, the US shipbuilding industry has produced defense vessels rather than cruise ships. The winds are changing: a shipbuilding contract for two cruise vessels has been announced by American Classic Voyages and Ingalls Shipyard (Miss.), a subsidiary of Litton Industries. Delta Queen Steamboat has contracted with Nichols Bros. Boat Builders, Inc. for the Columbia Queen and Atlantic Marine for two newbuilds for subsidiary Delta Queen Coastal Cruises. World City also plans to build at US shipyards.

The Phoenix World City Also Rises

[http://www.developmentchannel.com/content/ppho9712.htm]

Phoenix World City, Knut Kloster's dream of a 6,200-passenger floating city has a new lease on life, a new management partnership and a new name. Westin Hotels and Resorts has teamed up with Kloster to market and manage America World City: The Westin Flagship. Westin would manage the $1.2 billion 'floating hotel'.

World City has already secured $100 million in equity from strategic partners and is pursuing a US Department of Transportation Title 11 loan guarantee for 87 percent of the cost of the ship. An initial public offering in commercial stock has also been proposed, along with strategic equity agreements with partners like Westin.

Highlights of America World City: The Westin Flagship

- US built and staffed, the ship would be slightly larger than the biggest aircraft carrier afloat and two-and-a-half times bigger than any ship cur rently in development.

- Size? Nearly a quarter of a mile in length.

  - The ship will accommodate 6,200 guests in 2,800 rooms and suites.

  - 15 international restaurants.

  - Most staterooms would be in one of three hotel towers on the ship's deck.

  - The America World City would have its own marina with a fleet of four 400- passenger day-cruisers.

  - The vessel will become a meeting Mecca. Plans call for 100,000 square feet of function space. As the only major cruise ship sailing under the US flag, America World City would have a unique tax-deductible status.

  - The vessel would deploy in the Caribbean.

The project also includes a 90-acre development at Port Canaveral, Florida, as well as development of a Northeast cruise port at the 452-acre now defunct Military Ocean Terminal site in Bayonne, N.J.. At least two more floating cities are planned, one to cruise the West Coast and Hawaii, the other to sail in Asia.

Home away from home.

Surely the 50 room beach cottage and the mountainside estate will soon become passé. Soon you can purchase your own private getaway that really 'gets-away': a residence at sea aboard a luxury cruise ship.

The newest concept in cruising, World of ResidenSea is expected to enter service in April 2001, at which time she will embark on a three year fixed itinerary of world cruises.

It's no surprise that Knut Kloster, Jr. is the pioneer behind this project, along with other recognized cruise industry pros. The Kloster family started Norwegian Cruise Lines (NCL) and Knut Kloster, Jr. has served as chairman and CEO of both Royal Cruise Lines and NCL.

The World of ResidenSea also inherits the vision of the marine architects who designed the Seabourn Pride and Spirit, Silver Cloud, Silver Wind, Seabourn Goddess I and II and the Royal Viking Queen. The ship will be managed by Silversea Cruises Ltd. and will be built in Rissa, Norway by Fosen Mek. Verksteder A/S at an estimated cost of USD 262.5 million.

This 40,000-ton ship is expected to carry an average of 285 guests plus a crew of 252. ResidenSea expects guest/owners to be 40% Americans, 40% Europeans and 20% from other nations.

Money Talks

Choose from 110 'apartments' ranging from 1,100 square feet to 3,200 square feet in size. Prospective residents will have a choice of six floor plans including penthouses and bi-level residences. Each unit will feature two or three bedrooms, each with its own complete bathroom fully equipped kitchen; private terrace with whirlpool; walk-in closets; audio system; television and VCR; mobile phone; fax and a personal computer; built-in safe; and 24-hour security.

In addition, there will be 88-guest suites ranging in size from 220 to 500 square feet. Your new home will come stylishly decorated and furnished; complete with linen, china, cutlery and crystal.

Daily housekeeping service, repairs and replacement of appliances, fixtures and fittings supplied by the builder will be covered by an annual maintenance charge of between USD $60,000 to $240,000.

Two entire decks will be dedicated to a combination resort, street at sea, and a village of facilities. You'll find dining, entertainment, sports, shopping, business and leisure activities. There will be several restaurants and a number of lounges and bars, a casino, night club, and theater, as well as a library, museum, and business center. Your home at sea also sports a retractable marina, so bring the toys.

Oh - one mustn't forget: guests can take advantage of the "market room" with a licensed stock and bond broker and of course, the helicopter landing pad.

By Invitation Only.

Prices for World of ResidenSea homes range from USD $2,000,000 to $6,840,000 and they are being sold by invitation only.

Amenities and Services offered by the ResidenSea Club:

- Reciprocal privileges at private clubs around the world.

- Full-size indoor tennis court.

- Golf Academy with professional instructor; driving range and putting green.

- Swimming pools, whirlpools deck sports and water sports.

- Spa and Health and Fitness Center.

- 5 restaurants and a gallery of lounges, bars, and shops.

- Casino, nightclub, dancing, and cabaret.

- 150-seat theater/cinema.

- Wind-shielded outdoor garden.

- Rooms for private functions.

- Library, museum, art exhibitions, business center.

ResidenSea Itinerary 2001
The following itinerary is subject to change.

April - US, East Coast

May - US, East Coast, Channel Islands, England, North France

June - North France, North Spain, Holland, Belgium

July - Holland, Svalbard, Norway, North Cape

August - Baltic, Estonia, Sweden, Finland, Russia, Scotland

September - Scotland, Iceland, Greenland, England

October - Mediterranean, Spain, Sicily

November - Mediterranean, West Coast Africa, South Africa

December - South Africa, East Africa

Size and "One-upsman-ship"

Size: Super-Mega VS Boutique

Super-Mega ships	85,000 to 142,000 tons	2,112 to 3,114 passengers (pax).
Mega-ships	61,000 to 84,000 tons	1,500 to 2,112 pax.
Midsize ships	20,000-60,000 tons	500 to 1,500 pax.
Small/Boutique	20,000 grt	100 to 500 pax.

The next generation of newbuilds will be Mega and Super-mega ships or small boutique ships, with little in-between. Expect the game of 'one-upsman-ship' to continue as 3000+ passenger ships compete for the title of 'world's largest.' Another strong trend shows small or 'boutique' ships with 100-400 passengers capturing the soft adventure and ultra-luxe vacation market.

Is bigger better? Is less more?

Larger ships usually offer more activities, entertainment, children's programs and choice of discos, nightclubs and restaurants. Wide-open spaces and 10 deck high atrium areas do wonders for the resort vacation fan. There's sure to be something for all ages aboard these floating resorts.

Smaller ships (100-500 guests) have their own cache and offer a range of cruise experiences; unusual itineraries and specialty programs. These smaller ships provide two types of cruise vacations: exclusive, ultra-deluxe cruise vacations and hands-on, up-close soft adventure.

Do you prefer casual vacations with full-scale Broadway-style entertainment and 10,000 square-foot casinos? Are you more at home at black-tie soirees with country-club service? Or are you looking for a 'blue-jeans and binoculars' excursion to exotic ports the mega-liners can't reach?

Whatever your vacation style -- there's a ship; Super-Mega, Mega, Midsize or Boutique; and an itinerary for you. Use your *Cruise Chooser Personality Quiz* results and the following reviews to help match your own personality profile to the perfect ship.

Economies of Scale

For chief financial officers and shareholders, nothing could be finer than the profitable economies of scale achieved by building 2000-3000+ passenger mega/ super-mega ships. The newest ships are bigger, faster and full of surprises. The fleet of the future boasts entire decks dedicated to children's activities; alternative a-la-carte restaurants, Vegas-calibre casinos, expansive spas and ice skating rinks.

ONE **BIG** BOAT

Royal Caribbean International's Voyager of the Seas has raised the all-time record for most guests on a single cruise to 3,608 guests - a figure that included 380 honeymooners. Voyager of the Seas and its sistership, Explorer of the Seas will be joined by three more Voyager-class ships.

One foot too wide.

PANAMAX dimension standards enable Panama and Suez canal transits for worldwide deployment. Carnival's Destiny is one foot too wide for passage through the Panama Canal. Carnival Corporation's new Destiny-class ships carry 2,578-pax each and are "fabulously profitable."

At 159 feet wide, Princess Cruises' Grand Princess is also too 'beamy' for Panamax standards. Look for more 2,600 passenger Grand-class ships from Princess.

At 951 feet, Holland America Line's Rotterdam-class vessels will be among the longest passenger vessels in the world, but will still be able to transit the Panama Canal.

World's Largest?

Cunard's Queen Mary II is expected to be the largest passenger vessel ever built. Pricetag: $780 million US. The new liner will debut in 2003, sporting a classic design reminiscent of the grand dames of the past. Look for a dramatic raked prow, similar to QE2, a matte black-painted hull and a giant single stack, painted historic "Cunard Red" with black bands.

At more than 1100 feet long, her hull will be longer than three football fields-as long, in fact, as four city blocks-making her the longest passenger vessel ever built. Her power plant will produce sufficient electricity to light a city the size of Southampton, England. And her engines will produce a mighty 140,000 horsepower. Her great whistle will be audible from a distance of ten miles.

Queen Mary II

"The true nature of an ocean liner is that of a majestic thoroughbred roaming the oceans of the world. They are conceived with a long, streamlined hull, a proportionally long bow section and a stepped stern, giving them a sleek profile that is distinctive and pleasing to the eye. They are capable of very high speeds. The speed of Queen Mary II will probably not exceed that of Queen Elizabeth 2, Cunard's current flagship, which is the fastest deep sea passenger ship in the world. However, she will certainly be built to operate at speeds in the vicinity of 30 knots. She must therefore possess an inherent strength and stability necessary for high-speed passage through open ocean conditions, and a deep, narrow draft to cut the water for a comfortable and stable ride.

Modern cruise ships stick more closely to ports of call which they visit on an almost daily basis. The seagoing experiences are uniquely different. Certainly, there is a vast public for the cruise experience. We believe, similarly, there is an eager and growing audience for the drama, elegance and shipboard ambiance exemplified by sailing aboard a true Atlantic ocean liner.

We know that details of our liner are eagerly awaited but no one has built a true ocean liner in more than 30 years. It is nearly a lost art. Shipbuilders can't simply go into their plans files and pull out a convenient blueprint. We are recreating history." Larry Pimental, President, Cunard.

The liner will carry 2500 guests in dramatic palatial interior spaces, reminiscent of the White Star liner Titanic. Guests can meet and mingle their way through expansive promenades, elegant grand restaurants, gracious public rooms and grand staircases. Highlights include an onboard Maritime Museum of liner history; a pub with its own onboard micro-brewery; an advanced Computer Learning Center.

What dog were the fastest oceanliners compared to?

The Greyhound. Speedy Blue Riband winners were often referred to as the "greyhounds of the sea."

Royal Caribbean International's Voyager-Class sisterships to the popular Voyager of the Seas will continue to vie for the title of **"world's largest."** RCI's 142,000 grt Voyager-class ships carry an average of 3,114 passengers.

"World's Largest True Sail Ship,"

Royal Clipper, "World's Largest True Sail Ship," will set sail Spring, 2000 for its inaugural season in the Mediterranean. You can cross the ocean under sail, twice yearly, as the ship repositions from the Far East to the Eastern Mediterranean and on to the Eastern Caribbean.

At 439 feet, Royal Clipper is only the second sailing ship in history to be built fully-rigged with 5 masts and square sails on all 5 masts. The first was the Preussen, the 1902 flagship of Flying P lines. Nearly a century later, the modern Royal Clipper offers suites with whirlpools and private verandahs, a retractable water-sports platform and three on-deck swimming pools.

Hoist Mateys!

Strap on a safety harness and climb the 'rat-lines' to a lookout area mid-way up your choice of five masts. Royal Clipper bar staff can deliver champagne or other beverages to your perch. Your selection will be hoisted up to you by a block and tackle rig.

Highlights of the Small/Boutique Cruise Experience

Soft Adventure

Ecuador and Galapagos Island Cruises.

Cruise 600 miles west of Ecuador in the Pacific, aboard the Tropic Sun or another small ship, and you'll find the 48 islands and rocks of the Galapagos archipelago. Only 5 of the islands are populated. The animals and birds on these islands have no fear of man. You will never forget the many strange and familiar creatures you will be able to observe in their natural and totally undisturbed own world.

The Tropic Sun, originally built as a research vessel, has been converted to a small passenger ship since 1994 and renovated in 1998. Fellow passengers will likely be adventure travelers, vacationers, scuba divers, and snorkelers.

The vessel accommodates 40 passengers in 20 double occupancy cabins. All cabins are outside, have private bathrooms with showers, 3 x 4 ft picture windows and are air-conditioned. Two suites have private balconies. A special swim and dive platform allows easy access to the water and small boats.

Alaska's Glacier Bay Tours & Cruises

Alaska's Glacier Bay Tours & Cruises is a Native-owned Alaska cruise line specializing in adventure cruises and wilderness tours. These exclusive small ship cruises allow adventurers the unique opportunity to explore up close by sea kayaking and hiking on shore.

The line's Alaska's Inside Passage aboard the Wilderness Discoverer features guided shore excursions, Mendenhall River rafting tours and visits to the Alaskan Raptor Rehabilitation Center and American Bald Eagle Foundation.

The Executive Explorer's streamlined catamaran design allows for faster cruising and more time in port.

Visit a traditional Tlingit Indian village, watch for whales in Frederick Sound, and search for grizzlies along Admiralty Island. Guests sailing with the Wilderness Explorer have an opportunity to spend up to two days kayaking and hiking in spectacular Glacier Bay.

After the exhilaration of kayaking, hiking, wildlife observation and nature photography, return to your cruise ship 'base camp' to relax, share experiences, enjoy delicious meals, and sleep in comfort while the vessel positions you for the next day's adventure.

Because this unique charter vessel accommodates a mere 34 passengers, you travel with a small group of fellow adventurers, who, like you, are looking for an active and intimate experience in Alaska's pristine wilderness. Kayak and shore expeditions are limited to groups of 12 to minimize tourist impact on the environment. Each voyage is different because the itinerary can be adjusted to suit the interest of passengers, and to accommodate wildlife and glacier viewing opportunities.

Old Money

Heiress Marjorie Merriweather Post and financier E. F. Hutton spared no expense when they commissioned the largest private sailing ship ever built. In the 30s and 40s, the Sea Cloud hosted the Duke and Duchess of Windsor, Franklin D. Roosevelt and Sweden's King Gustavus V.. Fitted with 30 sails and staffed with 60 crew, the Sea Cloud caters to only 69 passengers on Mediterranean, Caribbean and Atlantic voyages. Snorkel, windsurf or water-ski from untrammeled beaches or take Zodiacs and tender boats ashore. The dining room accommodates all guests at one sitting; and beverages are complimentary with lunch and dinner. All cabins are air-conditioned and offer a safe, telephone, hair-dryer and bathrobes. Recent additions to the Sea Cloud fleet: Sea Cloud II and River Cloud II.

Live the Luxe Life
Seabourn Goddess I & II

The 'yacht-like' casual luxury experience found aboard Seabourn Goddess vessels was created to serve an affluent and discriminating travelers. The line's well-earned reputation for offering one of the most exclusive vacations in the world is built on a refined blend of personal attention, yacht-like elegance and a variety of amenities and services usually reserved for grand ocean liners. At just 4,250-tons, the ships accommodate 116 guests in 58 outside "suite-rooms."

Travel & Leisure compared the Dining Salon to a two-star Michelin restaurant, featuring international cuisine and offering leisurely dinners prepared to individual order during one sitting. All beverages are complimentary and tipping is discouraged. Sail in splendor to the Caribbean, Mediterranean or Transatlantic.

Silversea gets the Gold

Winner of "World's Best Small Cruise Line" in *Travel & Leisure's* World's Best Awards.

Aboard Silversea, the tangibles of ultra-luxury travel: Christofle silverware, Frette bed linens, soft down pillows and Bvlgari bath amenities; are subtly blended with an intangible at-your-service atmosphere to satisfy your every desire, 24-hours a day.

Whether you crave champagne and caviar on your private verandah, or an elegant dinner served course-by-course in your suite, you'll appreciate the impeccable service and attention to detail that have earned the line the industry's highest accolades.

At just 16,800-tons, Silver Cloud and Silver Wind cater to 296 guests on journeys to the world's intimate waterways and exotic destinations with voyages to the Mediterranean, Northern Europe, Africa/ India, South America, the Far East, Australia/New Zealand and Canada/New England.

Silversea's all-inclusive fares, feature all ocean-view suite accommodations (most with private verandah); round-trip air transportation with complimentary or reduced rate upgrades to Business Class airfare available on select itineraries; deluxe pre-cruise hotel accommodations; all beverages, including select wines and spirits; all gratuities; all port charges; transfers and portage and 'The Silversea Experience,' a special shore event offered on select itineraries.

B. **Trends in Accommodations, Public Areas, Facilities, Technology**

What's stands out aboard the newest ships? What are the latest trends in accommodations, public areas, facilities and technology? You'll be delighted ...

Balconies, verandahs & suites galore.

Be sure to pack extra sunscreen - you'll need it for sunny afternoons on your private balcony. For a majority of newbuilds, balconies or verandahs come standard with an outside stateroom. In keeping with this trend, a premium cruise line may convert existing picture windows to sliding glass French doors.

All-suite, all-balcony

Radisson Seven Seas Cruises has signed an agreement to build a new, all-suite, all-balcony, 720-guest luxury cruise ship scheduled for delivery in February 2001. The new ship will feature 280 standard ocean view suites of 28 square meters including balconies. An additional 80 suites will range from 35 to 100 square meters. Sistership Seven Seas Navigator's suites range from 301 to 1,173 square feet (including balcony), and offer walk-in closets and full bathrooms. While the Seven Seas Navigator is the cruise line's first all-suite ship (90 percent with private balconies), the newbuild will be its first all-balcony, all-suite vessel.

Reserve a suite aboard **Celebrity Cruises'** Millennium and enjoy these services and amenities: Welcome Aboard champagne, personalized stationery, a private portrait sitting, Celebrity tote bag, 100% cotton oversized bath towels, priority check-in and debarkation, express luggage delivery at embarkation, dining room seating preference, invitation to private art preview, opportunity to book in-suite massages.

Millennium suites also provide butler service, which includes: Full breakfast, lunch and dinner service in suites, evening hors d'oeuvres daily, complimentary espresso, and cappuccino, daily news delivery, in-suite afternoon tea service, assistance with packing and unpacking, shoeshine service, and delivery of requested board games.

Wow! Outside staterooms on Disney Cruise Lines' Wonder have two bathrooms! One with a sink and a second with sink, toilet and shower. Aboard Carnival's Destiny you can lounge in a steaming Jacuzzi - on your own private verandah. Quite a leap from cruising's humble beginnings, when there was no running water in cabins - only public bathing rooms.

11-deck-high atria, 2-story restaurants and bustling promenades...

See and be seen in cruising's first horizontal atrium aboard **Royal Caribbean International's** Voyager of the Seas. The Royal Promenade is the length of two football fields and four decks high with two 11 deck-high atria (The Centrums.) The Promenade is fashioned after London's Burlington Arcade with a wide selection of shops, restaurants and entertainment areas fronting on a winding street. Highlights include the world's largest interactive roulette wheel, activated by a four-deck-high roulette ball tower; and street festivities and performers.

The Voyager of the Seas also features inside staterooms with a view - a cruise ship first. These atrium-view staterooms have bay windows overlooking the Royal Promenade with great people-watching views of boutiques and restaurants.

Carnival Cruise Lines' Carnival Triumph features a towering nine-deck-high glass-enclosed atrium. The Carnival Pride boasts a two-level main restaurant for all guests, and two consecutive decks of bars, lounges and nightspots, one with an outdoor wrap-around promenade.

Meet me at the Spa.

A oasis for both body and mind awaits you in **Celebrity Cruises'** AquaSpas. Schedule your appointments the first day of your voyage and enjoy the revitalizing powers of the sea with hydro-based treatments. Onboard the Century, Galaxy and Mercury, guests may experience a 10,000-square-foot spa environment that includes a 115,000-gallon Thalassotherapy pool with a choice of stimulating water therapies to ensure complete mental relaxation. You'll be transported body and soul: enjoy the best of Eastern and Western meditation and spa therapies in at atmosphere reminiscent of traditional Japanese bathouses and opulent Moorish architecture.

Various modalities of massage and personal fitness training sessions are also available. The spa treatment programs are custom-designed by Steiner Leisure Ltd. of London.

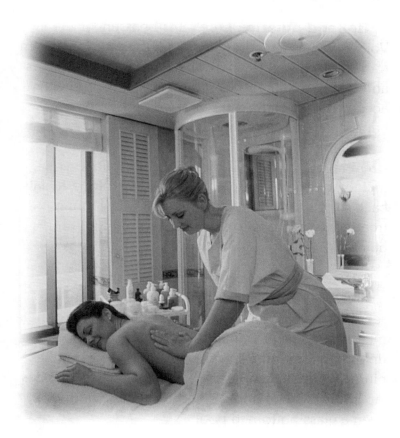

Ship Shape

Every **Royal Caribbean** ship has its own custom designed solarium and spa facilities. Invigorate yourself in state-of-the-art fitness centers, take an exercise class or renew your spirit in the spa. Pamper yourself with a facial massage or mudbath. Get set for an evening of glamour with complete salon services: hair styling, manicure and pedicure and makeovers.

Holland America Line's 1440-passenger Volendam has increased its spa treatment rooms from four to six. All treatment rooms have private showers and toilets; two of the six spa treatment rooms will accommodate wet treatments such as hydrotherapy baths, seaweed wraps and mud treatments.

Holland America's Steiner-operated spas offer stress relief treatments and fitness consultations including aromatherapy massage, reflexology, facials, back stress relief programs, Ionithermie slimming treatments, personal training, fitness analysis and hair and manicure services.

Water, Water Everywhere: Pools

Guests aboard today's newbuilds may share the sense of novelty experienced by cruisers aboard the maiden voyage of Cunard's Aquitania. In 1914, the first shipboard indoor pool opened. This new millennium will treat passengers to a variety of water slides, lap pools, wading pools, solarium pools, whirlpools; even a glass-bottomed pool.

Freestyle Dining on the Royal Clipper

Three decks above the atrium and dining room; the ceiling is a glass-bottomed pool! Watch the swimmers above you burn calories while you order a second helping of baked Alaska.

Pack extra swimsuits for the Carnival Triumph's seven whirlpools and four swimming pools - one with a 214-foot-long twisting, turning water slide!

Fun Design Features

Kids big and small might find themselves taking an few extra rides on **Holland America Line's** Zaandam's 'exterior elevators.' The outside elevators on both port and starboard decks offer 10 decks worth of panoramic views.

Fans of Route 66 can get their kicks aboard **Disney Cruise Line's** Wonder. 1950's-era billboards, road map carpeting and highway light poles guide guests along Route 66 from nightclub to lounge to comedy club.

Technology at your fingertips.

Technology fans, computer users and Internet junkies are the winners in the cruise industry's 'techno- battle of the seas.' Here are some of the developments in shipboard high-tech:

Stay in touch with friends and family from your in-stateroom Internet/e-mail data ports aboard **Holland America Line's** Rotterdam-class vessels.

Princess Cruises' Grand Princess' offers a 'motion-based' virtual reality theater and a 'blue screen' backdrop where you can star in your own video.

Carnival Cruise Lines' virtual-reality machines allow players to compete in virtual combat. Movement is tracked by video headsets to determine the scenery and challenges.

RCI's Voyager of the Seas' Conference Center seats up to 400 guests, and converts into six large breakout rooms. Look for a multi-media screening room, wireless control of audio-visual equipment, sound, light, and room temperature; and tele-video conferencing facilities. The state-of-the-art La Scala Theater brings hi-tech Broadway style productions to sea with a hydraulic-powered rising orchestra pit.

C. Trends in Activities, Programs & Entertainment

Take advantage of fun activities and programs as cruise lines outdo each other with new theme cruises, celebrity guests, expert lecturers, fun gimmicks and phenomenal facilities.

There's plenty to do onboard whether you lounge poolside or practice your golf game on the putting green. Sports facilities on today's ships have expanded way beyond ping pong and shuffleboard. Now you can play tennis, basketball and volleyball. Days at sea are filled with a range of activities, from traditional cruise pastimes such as bingo and passenger talent shows to ice skating and rock climbing.

Rock-climbing in the Middle of the Caribbean?

Royal Caribbean International's Voyager of the Seas has a thirty-foot rock wall mounted on the ship's funnel - two hundred feet above sea level. Climbing equipment and novice lessons are provided. The Voyager of the Seas also offers full-court basketball, an in-line skating track, a golf simulator and a 9-hole putting green.

It's your turn!

Now that World Champion Figure Skating legends Katarina Witt, Robin Cousins, Brian Orser, and Todd Eldredge have sliced the ice of the world's first permanent floating ice rink, its your turn. Skate your heart out aboard the Voyager of the Seas, that's what Brian Boitano would do. Located in the 900-seat Studio B, the ice rink is part of a multi-purpose entertainment complex that will feature open skating, spectacular ice shows by professional skaters year-around and celebrity skaters on select sailings. (Yes, they have a Zamboni.)

Ice carving too...

Holland America's hostess demonstrations introduce the art of ice carving, vegetable and melon carving, origami, napkin folding and scarf tying and 'how to' workshops for making marzipan and famous Dutch cheese fondue.

Get in a workout.

Royal Caribbean International's ShipShape fitness activities include low and high impact aerobics, an on-deck jogging track, basketball hoops, step and stretch classes, free weights, Lifecycle, treadmill and other cardio machines.

Sample Lectures and Workshops

Join **Holland America Line's** hosts for an art and history tour of your ship's art and antiques collection, worth approximately $2 million per ship.

National Geographic journalists and photographers will share their personal travel experiences with **Silversea Cruises** passengers during *National Geographic Traveler* voyages. See the world through their eyes with lectures, slide presentations and discussions.

Attend wine-themed seminars and tastings as you visit some of Europe's most famous wine regions. Norwegian Cruise Line's Wine and Romance voyages aboard the Norway has brought aboard experts such as Joseph Ward, wine editor at *Conde Nast Traveler*, Malcolm Gluck, wine correspondent for The Guardian, and Jilly Goolden, host of the BBC program "Food and Drink." Sail from Barcelona to Southampton. Visit Florence, Pisa, Palma de Mejorca, Malaga, Lisbon, Bordeaux Le Havre.

Even at sea, "Men are from Mars, Women are from Venus," and **Carnival Cruise Lines** has invited certified facilitators to present Mars-Venus Workshops aboard select sailings. Based on Dr. John Gray's best-selling series of books, Men are from Mars, Women are from Venus; these entertaining workshops feature Gray's video seminars, exercises and discussion. Prices for scheduled sailings include the workshop, champagne & chocolates!

Royal Olympic Cruises' Maya Equinox cruise features a complimentary full day tour to Chichen Itza, timed to coincide with the vernal equinox. The yearly 'return of the sun serpent' is just one of the fascinating aspects of Maya culture presented in lectures, round-table discussions and casual conversations with renowned archaeologists, historians, and astronomers. Previous on-board specialists include Dr. Anthony Aveni, Dr. Edwin C. Krupp, Dr. Tom Bopp, Tim W. Kuzniar, M. Scott Carpenter, Phyllis Burton Pitluga, Darien D. Gould, Dr. Rebecca Storey, George T. Keene and Dr. Randolph Widmer. The Maya itinerary features fascinating ports-of-call: Isla de Roatan, Honduras; Cozumel, Mexico; Puerto Cortes, Honduras; Playa del Carmen, Mexico; Belize City, Belize.

Broaden your vocabulary aboard a **Holland America Line** cruise. Spanish language instruction is available on all Caribbean cruises, and introductory Dutch language classes on most cruises.

Join Bridge lecturers as they tip their hand and share winning strategies on Holland America voyages of 10 days or more.

D. **Trends in Dining**

Anything you'd like - anyway you like it - anytime!

A majority of today's floating resorts are supplementing the formal Titanic-style dining experience with a variety of menu choices, dining times and themed settings. With more than 55 new ships joining the worldwide fleet, you'll find satisfying menu choices for children, vegetarians, gourmets, meat-

and-potato lovers and health-conscious diners. You'll also have your choice of dining times and restaurant themes. Feel like lingering over sushi and steak at a Japanese restaurant? Want a quick-n-easy pizza? (Open 24-hours) You'll find more ships are offering new dining options, plus the traditional 5-course feast served promptly at 6 and 8 p.m..

First or Second Seating?

Many cruise lines ask you to choose between first and second seating (6 p.m. and 8 p.m.) for meals in the main dining rooms. For more tips on seating time selection, see *Cruising Made Easy*.

Trendsetters in dining options.

Disney Cruise Line's unique 'rotation dining' gives guests an opportunity to experience a new restaurant nightly, while receiving continuing personal attention from the same waiter. You and your tablemates 'rotate' to a different restaurant each evening - and your waiter comes with you. Enjoy French, California-contemporary and Caribbean cuisine. Disney also offers a Northern Italian restaurant for adults-only.

Crystal Cruises Crystal Harmony and Crystal Symphony feature specialty restaurant experiences including traditional Japanese cuisine at Kyoto on Crystal Harmony, and innovative Asian cuisine prepared with a contemporary flair at Jade Garden on Crystal Symphony. Both ships offer Old World charm and authentic regional Italian cuisine at Prego. There is no additional charge for dining in these specialty restaurants.

Visit Crystal Cruises' Web site for a Virtual Reality tour of the Crystal Dining Room, Kyoto, Jade Garden and Prego. [http//:www.crystalcruises.com]

Royal Caribbean International's, Eagle-class ships offer a variety of dining options. The spectacular Voyager of the Seas three-level main dining room has separate themed dining areas; Carmen, La Boheme and Magic Flute; interconnected by a dramatic three-deck grand staircase. The adjoining Seville and Granada dining rooms are available for smaller parties.

Other dining opportunities include: Café Promenade, for continental breakfast, all-day pizzas and specialty coffees; Island Grill, for casual dinner, without reservations, featuring freshly grilled entrees and a display kitchen; Portofino, an upscale Euro-Italian restaurant, for dinner with reservations and SeaSide Diner, a 1950s 24-hour eatery featuring jukebox hits and indoor/outdoor seating.

What next, waitresses on roller-skates? Royal Caribbean International has teamed up with Johnny Rockets restaurant to offer its popular 40s - 50s style hamburger-malt shop onboard the first Voyager-class vessel, Voyager of the Seas. Johnny Rockets' features a retro-styled burger-malt shop environment complete with vintage memorabilia, singing and dancing waiters and tabletop jukeboxes that still cost only a nickel.

Casual dining is the goal at **Carnival Cruise Lines**' Seaview Bistros, which feature flexible evening dining from 6-9:30 p.m. on the Lido deck - no reservations required. Guests can enjoy a light fare of soups, salads, pastas as well as steaks cooked to order and desserts. This cafe-like dining choice also offers a daily chef's special; and a wide selection of wines by the glass, bottle or carafe.

Carnival's fleetwide 24-hour pizzerias serve seven different kinds of pizza and calzone, along with garlic bread and Caesar salad.

Carnival's casual dining options complement full-service meals available in the main dining rooms. Don't pass up the late night buffet - tempting hot and cold appetizers, salads, meats carved to order, nightly specialty items and scrumptious desserts.

Worried you'll gain 10 pounds?
Try Royal Caribbean International's ShipShape menu on for size:

Appetizers

Tuna Fish with Olives and Onions • Fresh Tropical Fruit Cocktail
Pineapple Gondola Cranberry Juice • Melon Pearls au Porto
Mango Nectar • Tomato Stuffed with Baby Shrimp

Soups

Consommé Doble al Jerez • Beef Broth and Tropical Vegetables
Clear Oxtail Amontillado • Chilled Cucumber Doria
Chilled Vichyssoise • Consommé Celestine • Ginger Chicken

Salads

Salade Printaniere Monte Carlo • Hawaiian Salad
Suzy Wong Salad • Ensalada Cataline

Entrees

Red Snapper Cantonese • Poached Alaskan King Salmon
Rigatoni Primavera • Cornish Game Hen Ajillo
Cajun Fried Catfish • Roast Vermont Turkey • Coq au Vin
Supreme of Boston Sole, Madagascar • Golden Fried Lemon Sole
Broiled Swordfish Steak • Broiled Chicken Djionnaise
Stuffed Flounder Primavera • Mahi Mahi Fillet Meuniere

Desserts

Chocolate Soufflé with Amaretto Sauce
Sherbet • Wisconsin Apple Strudel • Cranberry Chiffon Pie
Pineapple Meringue Pie • Almond Apple Pie
Tropical Fruit Strudel

Heed the Call of the Chime Master

A polite doorman opens the door and invites you to dine at Holland America Line's Lido deck. Listen closely! The dining hour is discreetly heralded throughout the ship's public rooms by a steward/chime master playing melodious chimes.

Health-conscious vacationers will appreciate **Carnival's** Nautica Spa Fare, delicious guilt-free dishes available on all menus. (Designated by a special symbol as lower in fat, cholesterol, sodium and calories.) Meats, fish and poultry are broiled or roasted, salads come with low-fat free dressings and desserts are made with sugar substitutes.

Decisions! Decisions! Meat, Fowl or Fish? Red or White? Steamed or Poached? Au jus or chutney?

Too many choices!? When the mind-boggling array of delicious cuisine begins to puzzle you - Ask the Maitre d'!

With an average of 20 years of experience with cruise cuisine, he's sure to recommend a few favorites. Maitre d's often begin their careers as waiters, buffet stewards or assistant bartenders. Working closely with a multi-cultured staff, the Maitre d's masterpiece is a seam-less dining room experience. The Maitre d's goal? Guests will talk about this cruise for a lifetime.

> **Princess Cruises' Maitre d's recommend:**
> Italian native Balbiani Anbelo adores the Princess Love Boat Dream, a lovely dessert created by Giovanni, the chief baker on Regal Princess.
>
> Tinonin Elia's favorites are Beef Wellington, Rack of Lamb, Crepes Suzette and Tiramisu.
>
> Pasta Arrabiata hits the spot for Giorgio Pisano, 24 year Princess veteran.
>
> Top choices for Rui G.R. Pereira, of Lisbon, Portugal are Rack of Lamb and Grand Marinier Soufflé.

Tips for the Vegetarian Cruiser.

Vegetarian selections are available aboard a majority of ships. Consult your travel agent before booking. Introduce yourself to your Maitre d' at a non-peak hour - you'll find he is more than accom-modating of your dietary requests. Creativity and variety of vegetarian selections varies. See the *Best of*

the *Best Awards* at **www.cruisechooser.com**.

resources: books

Vegetarian Traveler, Civic, Jed and Susan Civic, ISBN: 0943414795

resources: agencies and tour operators

resources: tour operators & associations

Vegetarian Journeys, 2067 Constitution Boulevard, Sarasota, FL 34321 (941) 927-1255.

[http://www.vegetarianjourneys.com].

Green Earth Travel, 6505 Democracy Boulevard, Bethesda, MD 20817 (888) 246-8343, (301) 571-4603.

[http://www.vegtravel.com].

Vegetarian Travel Board [http://www.veg.org].

Travel recommendations for and by vegetarians.

Order Your Favorite Royal Caribbean Recipes:

Order your favorite Royal Caribbean Recipes:

Minestrone Milanese, Chicken Coq au Vin, Scalloped Potatoes with Cheese, Ratatouille.

These recipes work beautifully whether you're feeding six hundred or just six. For a listing of additional menus and 37 scrumptious recipes for sale, send a check for $5.00, along with your name, address and zip code to:

Royal Caribbean Cruises
1050 Caribbean Way
Miami, FL 33132
Food Operations-MI-FO (Recipes)

Princess Cruises galleys
are staffed with as many as 150 hard-
working folks working round-the-clock
throughout the fleet, preparing approximately
15,000 meals and snacks daily.

Aboard Holland America Line's ships, the ratio
of dining room stewards to guests is 1:10. Two
dining room stewards work in a team with an
assistant dining room steward and a
head steward to assure the highest
quality service.

E. Trends in Itineraries, Ports of Departure, Destinations, Shore Excursions

Caribbean Winters, Alaskan Summers...and so much more.

55 new ships plus efforts to satisfy and retain experienced repeat passengers prompt cruise lines to develop more " exotic" itineraries and new ports of departure. Watch for sailings to Africa, Southeast Asia, South America, the South Pacific and India; plus new 'home ports' of departure. You'll also find more 'soft adventure,' voyages and specialty or age-specific shore excursions.

How are ports-of-call chosen?

Prime considerations for including a destination on an itinerary include passenger demand, ship design and tourism infrastructure.

Itinerary planners must consider the following:
• Can the ship travel fast enough to offer a port-per-day or more time in port?

• Is the ship small enough, or does it have a shallow draft allowing visits to less developed destinations?

• How will the itinerary appeal to passengers? Is it salable? Is there a supporting tourism infrastructure, such as dockage facilities, passenger terminals, ground transportation, air service and shore excursion companies?

• Can the port handle larger ships and greater numbers of passengers?

• Are there appropriate "home" ports of departure from which to begin the voyage?

Developing and Enhancing "Home" Ports

Competition for cruise line business intensifies as port authorities worldwide invest in infrastructure and promotion. Here are some examples of what it takes to get in the game.

Seattle's Bell Street Pier Vs Vancouver.

After 10 years of negotiations, Seattle's port commission voted to build a $12.7-million passenger ship terminal near the popular waterfront Pier 66 shopping and entertainment area. Bell Street Pier is positioned as an alternative homeport for the Alaska cruise market - heretofore dominated by Vancouver. Obstacles to development ranged from federal restrictions on foreign-flag passenger ships, to funding for facilities and marketing.

Currently 32 cruise ships call at Bell Street Pier, and the port is expected to handle at least 116,000 annual passengers compared with 7,000 in 1999. Bell Street was chosen as the homeport for Royal Caribbean International's Vision of the Seas summer cruises in the Pacific Northwest and Norwegian Cruise Line's first summer Alaskan sailings.

Port Canaveral, Disney Style

Disney Cruise Lines' Art Deco cruise ship terminal in Port Canaveral, Florida welcomes a dedicated fleet of buses transporting passengers from Walt Disney World resorts or the Orlando International Airport.

Long Beach

Carnival Corporation plans to construct and operate a new cruise ship terminal in the city of Long Beach, Calif. The new terminal will be built adjacent to the Queen Mary attraction and hotel, and is slated for completion in early 2001.

As the new homeport for the West Coast- based ships of the company's Carnival Cruise Lines division, the facility will include a single cruise berth

large enough to accommodate vessels the size of
Carnival Cruise Lines' 102,000-ton "Destiny-class"
series; and a 1,200 vehicle parking garage.

Port of Tampa

Tampa's proximity to the Western Caribbean and
Mexico, plus nearby popular attractions (Walt Disney
World, the Gulf beaches, Busch Gardens, Florida
Aquarium, and Tampa Bay Devil Rays and
Buccaneers) continue to draw cruise business.

Currently two lines operate from Tampa, Carnival
Cruise Lines and Holland America. Guests can spend
time pre- or post-cruise, shopping, dining or taking in
the latest movies at pier-side Seaport Center. Tampa's
reputation for convenience has been further
enhanced with the $6.5 million renovation to
Terminal 2. The facility doubled in size and an
enhanced passenger embarkation / disembarkation
area and multi-deck parking garage make Tampa one
of the easiest ports to sail from.

Tampa stands ready to take advantage of three
positive trends: fleet expansion (55 new ships by
2005) repeat cruisers demand for diverse itineraries
and the potential re-opening of Cuba to US travelers.

Popular Puerto Rico

Could Puerto Rico's Ricky Martin campaign be
paying off in more port calls?

'Shake it Ricky! You're so fine!' squealed travel
agents as they watched Ricky's promotional com-

mercial for Puerto Rico. Consumer demand for more port-intensive Caribbean itineraries coupled with the island's strategic location attracted more than one dozen lines in 1999.

Singapore

Singapore's $28 million cruise terminal complex and massive promotional efforts are spearheading Pacific Asia's entry into the global leisure cruise market. See the Cruise Guide to Destinations for Pacific-Asian itineraries.

Pacific Asia

Will the Pacific Asia region grow into a strong cruise market?

Itineraries showcasing Asian destinations are gaining in popularity, as US travelers move from tried-and-true Alaskan and Caribbean voyages to test unfamiliar waters. Asian travelers are also cruising more and investments by cruise companies and port authorities are higher than ever.

Star Cruises is one of the five largest cruise lines in the world and by year 2005, will have a fleet of 12 vessels sailing from Singapore, Port Klang, Phuket, Bangkok, Hong Kong, Taipei and Osaka/Kobe. During its first five years, Star Cruises carried more than 1 million passengers.

218

Port of Miami

The Port of Miami's latest addition is a new multi-million-dollar, 250,000-square-foot terminal constructed specially to accommodate Royal Caribbean International's Voyager of the Seas. The terminal is designed to expedite the boarding and disembarking process for up to 8,400 guests with spacious check-in areas and hospitality suites for relaxation or last-minute business conferences.

Cruisers will appreciate state-of-the-art security and baggage handling systems, plus secured covered parking for 733 cars in a four-story garage. The terminal features a series of sail-like structures that rise high above the two-story roofline and is crowned by a replica of Royal Caribbean's Viking Crown Lounge.

Trends in Shore excursions

Look for more active, interest-specific and age-specific shore excursions in addition to shopping excursions and popular sightseeing tours.

Black diamond or bunny slope?

Many cruise lines rate their shore excursions according to level of aerobic difficulty or physical exertion required. Carnival Cruise Lines rates their Alaskan shore excursions in three activity levels-- "easy," "moderate," and "adventure/considerable" -- to help guests determine which tour best suits their physical condition.

In Search of "soft" adventure.

Explore your world - conveniently! Soft-adventure cruises are catering to the experienced traveler who wants to visit new and exotic locales from the comfort and safety of a home-base cruise ship. See the Yangtze without the hassle of local hotels, get closer to the Galapagos aboard your ship's fleet of Zodiacs. Cross the Amazon rainforest by rope hanging bridges. All this and more - it's adventure made easy by the increasing number of 'expedition' cruise companies. Look to Lindblad Expeditions for the newest itineraries and unique programs in soft-adventure cruising.

Radisson Seven Seas Cruises' 170-passenger Hanseatic's "Indian Ocean Odyssey" joins up with Lifelong Learning to offer lectures and workshops with naturalists, and other experts from scientific organizations. Guests explore exotic mammals, birds and plants on their voyage from Capetown, South Africa to Madagascar.

Shore excursions created 'Just for Kids'

"Step right up, see the largest gold nugget in the world," is just one popular feature of **Holland America Line's** educational adventures geared to "Tween" cruisers on Alaskan voyages.

Tweens (ages 6-12) and teens (13-18) have their own kind of fun, accompanied by a Holland America Line youth coordinator or naturalist. Extreme Sports

Fans will enjoy the Dyea Mountain Bike and Float Adventure: a mountain-bike ride to historic Dyea and raft trip on the gentle Taiya River. Included are bikes, helmets, raingear, boots, lifejackets and a light snack, as well as round-trip transportation from the dock.

Teens suitup in rainwear and lifejackets for the Sitka Sea Kayaking adventure. Knowledgeable instructors coach them on safety and steering and they're off - in search of brown bear, Sitka black-tailed deer, harbor seals or sea otters. The 3-hour tour includes a hot beverage, snack and transfer back to town.

Local Flavor

Bangkok: Sign up for a Theravada Buddhist meditation class at the World Fellowship of Buddhists. Classes are offered every Sunday. *Hong Kong*: Gaze into your future at Fortune Teller's Alley

Trends in Destinations

Look for more diverse itineraries as cruise lines add new destinations to satisfy sophisticated cruisers.

Now Open for Business: Saudi Arabia.

The once off-limits Kingdom can now be toured via Lindblads Special Expeditions 15-day "Journey to Saudi Arabia" travel program. Get to know the history and culture of Saudi Arabia, beginning with a tour of the capital of Riyadh. Highlights include visits to the oil-producing region of Dhahran, the ancient city of Sakaka and the northern oasis of Domat Al-Jandal. A knowledgeable historian, regional expert and expedition leader will accompany guests throughout the journey.

Can't decide where to go? Try a World Cruise!

Holland America Line's, Year 2000 Grand World Voyage fulfills the ultimate wish list for Century Club Members seeking more stamps for their passports. This 96-day odyssey aboard the Rotterdam includes new ports and ports not visited in ten years by Holland America Line. The Rotterdam will visit 40 locations on five continents as it circumnavigates the globe.

The Grand World Voyage visits these ports: Georgetown, Grand Cayman; Manta, Ecuador; General San Martin (Pisco), Peru; Coquimbo (La Serena), Chile; Puerto Montt, Chile; Ushuaia Tierra del Fuego, Argentina; Buenos Aires, Argentina; Durban, South Africa; Zanzibar, Tanzania; Victoria, Seychelles; Male, Maldives; Madras, India; Singapore; Hong Kong; Xingang, PRC; Cheju City Cheju Island, South Korea; Kagoshima, Japan; Tokyo; Honolulu; Oahu; Kona; Hawaii; Balboa, Panama; Callao Per Arica,

Chile; Valparaiso, Chile; Experanza Station, Antarctic Peninsula; Cape Town, South Africa; Nosy B, Madagascar; Mombassa, Kenya La Digue and Praslin, Seychelles; Cochin, India; Phuket, Thailand; Vung Tau, Vietnam; Shanghai, PRC; Dalian, PRC; Nagasaki; Osaka; Midway Island; Lahaina, Maui; and Los Angeles.

Is cruising environmentally sound?
Then and Now.

Then: 1992 Princess Cruises' ships caught tossing plastic trash bags overboard, fined $500,000.

Now: Planet Princess

Princess Cruises has been awarded the US Coast Guard's William M. Benkert Award for excellence in marine environmental protection. The line's Planet Princess program was honored as the most comprehensive environmental program designed to reduce waste, conserve resources and educate employees.

The Benkert Award recognizes vessels and facility operators with marine environmental programs that exceed mere compliance with regulatory standards. The Coast Guard award recognizes Princess Cruises' superior level of environmental commitment and well-defined, dynamic environmental policy, which involves the participation of all employees.

In addition to the Benkert Award, Princess Cruises also recently received the ASTA/Smithsonian Magazine Environmental Award for environmental excellence, the British Airways Environmental Award for sustainable tourism and the Pacific Asia Tourist Association (PATA) Green Leaf Award.

Then: 1999, Royal Caribbean International, (RCI) fined for improper disposal of bilge water and 'gray-water.' The US Department of Justice concluded a five-year investigation into Royal Caribbean International's past environmental practices and RCI agreed to pay $18 million in fines, in addition to a recently paid $9 million penalty. RCI will also under-go five years of probation. Most of the violations occurred in 1994 and 1995.

Now: RCI strengthens its zero- tolerance policy toward environmental violations. Many of the com-pany's own initiatives were incorporated into an Environmental Compliance Program (ECP), which was part of the settlement agreement reached with the Justice Department. Here's an example of what RCI has achieved:
   • Developed and installed a state-of-the art filter-ing system that cleans bilge water three times more effectively than required by law.
   • Assigned each ship an environmental officer, who monitors shipboard environmental procedures.
   • Hired a new senior vice president of safety and

environment, who oversees overall environmental compliance and reports directly to the president assembled a new management team in marine operations, the division accountable for onboard environmental practices.

• Initiated comprehensive environmental audits conducted by outside consultants.

• All RCI Millennium-class vessels, along with their Vantage-class ships; will be among the first cruise ships to incorporate gas turbine propulsion. This technology minimizes environmental impact by reducing air emissions, sludge and oil waste.

MARPOL

The International Convention for the Prevention of Pollution from Ships (MARPOL) sets strict regulatory standards to prevent ship-generated waste. This legislation regulates water discharge, air quality, onboard solid waste management and recycling on all vessels.

Compact it, burn it or stow it? Let's hope the cruise industry doesn't "waste" any opportunities to be enviro-friendly. Ships worldwide face the challenge of balancing bottom lines and environmental responsibilities. The Eco-violence committed on our oceans is not limited to the above-mentioned incidents or companies. Cruise company leaders promise it won't happen again and perhaps their enhanced environmental programs will lead the way to a litter-free Gulf Stream.

Now you see it -- now you don't.

"These are sites that define the history and the humanity of the peoples of the world. Once these sites are lost, they are gone forever." Bonnie Burnham, president, World Monuments Fund.

On your next cruise, visit one of the 100 Most Endangered Sites on the World Monument's Watch. This list identifies cultural heritage sites that are urgently at risk and seeks funds for their rescue. A panel of nine experts identify additional sites yearly. Sites on the 2000 List of 100 Most Endangered Sites include Machu Picchu in Peru, Teotihuacán in Mexico, and an 8000-year-old rock art site in Niger.

For the Current Cumulative List of 100 Most Endangered Sites visit [http://www.worldmonuments.org]

For more information on the World Monuments Watch, please contact the World Monuments Fund, 949 Park Avenue New York, NY 10028.

From Afghanistan to Zimbabwe - sites to see:

A Sample of Endangered Sites
San Geronimo Fort, Portobelo and San Lorenzo Castle, Colon, Panama.

San Lorenzo Castle and Fort San Geronimo remain to testify to British and Spanish competition for domination over Caribbean basin colonies. The evolving architecture of these shoreline forts reveal Italian, French and Spanish influences.

Teotihuacán Archaeological Site, San Juan Teotihuacán, Mexico.
Once one of the world's largest cities; renamed Teotihuacán by the Aztecs, meaning "where the gods were born." Previous inappropriate conservation techniques along with inadequate monitoring and maintenance have left unique mural paintings at risk.

Morgan Lewis Sugar Mill, St. Andrew, Barbados
The last surviving wind-powered sugar-cane crushing mill in the Caribbean; all original working parts intact. The Morgan Lewis Sugar Mill symbolizes the huge fortunes built by the one-time slave labor-powered Caribbean sugar industry.

Valley of the Kings, Thebes, Luxor, Egypt.
Where nearly all of Egypt's New Kingdom pharaohs including Tutankhamen, Seti I and Rameses II are buried. The greatest threat is posed by a total failure to control rapidly increasing numbers of tourists who inflict considerable damage to the decorated tomb walls.

Machu Picchu, Urubamba, Cusco, Peru.
The 15th-century ancient Inca city is threatened
by a government-endorsed plan that seeks to build
a cable-car lift from Aguas Calientes below the site
to Machu Picchu which could destroy the serene,
isolated quality of the site and lead to a quadrupling
of visitors.

Old Bridge, Spanish Town, St. Catherine, Jamaica
'She waited for her lover to cross from Kingston to
Spanish Town.' Recently closed for preservation, this
cast-iron footbridge is considered the first of its kind
in the Americas. Built of prefabricated iron structure
made in England, and assembled on-site, it spans
nearly 82 feet across the Rio Cobre.

Tanah Lot Temple, Tabanan, Bali, Indonesia.
The Gods of the Sea are honored in the Tanah Lot
Temple. One hundred concrete tetrapods were
installed along the shoreline as a way to protect
some structures from the rise of the sea, however,
this greatly compromises the aesthetic integrity of
the temple and site.

National Art Schools, Cubanacán, Havana, Cuba.
Chronic poor maintenance and ill-conceived
additions have greatly compromised the schools for
modern dance, plastic arts, dramatic arts, music
and ballet.

San Juan De Ulua Fort, Veracruz, Mexico

San Juan de Ulua marks the site of the beginning of Spanish domination in Mexico. Juan de Grijalva discovered the island for Spain, in 1518, and construction of the fort began in 1535. Fort San Juan de Ulua protected the first port in the Americas; and by the eighteenth century, held the greatest concentration of riches in the Americas

Bermuda-invitation only.

This island of pink sand beaches is one of the most closely controlled and expensive (for the cruise lines,) ports-of-call in cruising. Bermuda's proximity to the US east coast and her popularity with New Yorkers and New Englanders allows the island bargaining powers Caribbean islands only dream of. A limited number of ships are issued landing permits during the prime summer season, between May and October. While many Caribbean ports eagerly court cruise business, the cruise lines must compete for Bermuda's five-year contracts.

Cuba

Will Cuba reopen to US travelers in your lifetime?

If the US re-instates American travel to Cuba, the cruise lines could capitalize on a whole new central Caribbean itinerary, with calls at Cuba, Jamaica, the Dominican Republic and Haiti.

Cuban cruises are already popular with Canadians and Europeans. **Costa Crociere's** Costa Playa has attracted cruisers from Britain, Italy, Germany, Spain, France, South America and Switzerland on sailings around the island's southern end. Departing from Cienfuegos, the Costa Playa called at Santiago de Cuba, Cayo Largo del Sur, Grand Cayman and Montego Bay.

Costa Crociere owns a 50% stake of Silares Terminales Caribe, a joint venture with the Cuban government, which operates three cruise terminals in Cuba. Silares Terminales Caribe invested $5.8 million in building a passenger terminal in Havana with two large vessel berths. The venture has an option to renovate four other Cuban berths: two in Havana, one in Mariel and one in Santiago de Cuba.

Cuba Cruise Corporation is the first North American company to market Nassau-Havana cruises to Americans. A bomb threat called off inaugural sailings.

Vist Cuba by video!
Resources:
"*For Love or Country*"
"*Dance with Me*"
"*Buena Vista Social Club*"
"*Chocolate and Strawberry*"

Destinations
Resources: Internet
Virtual Cities [http://www.virtualcities.com]
Lonelyplanet [http://www.lonelyplanet.com/]
Adventurous Traveler Bookstore
[http://www.adventuroustraveler.com]
Great Outdoors Recreation Pages
[http://www.gorp.com]

It's a cruise industry first!
There's a hot new zip code in town and it belongs
to Royal Caribbean International's Voyager of the
Seas: 33132-2028.

PART 6

Postcards from the Past

- ◆ **A Brief Glance at Cruising's History**

- ◆ **Firsts in Cruising**

Highlights of the Cruise Industry's Evolution

A brief history of cruising: from commercial vessels providing distribution, delivery, immigration and transportation; to the golden age of luxury ocean-liners and today's 'floating resort' cruise ships.

As your ship sets sail, wave Bon voyage and celebrate. You're now part of the rich heritage of passenger shipping. Everything that makes up your cruise today - from ship design and decor to destinations - was influenced by those who sailed before you: shipping magnates and merchants; emigrants and explorers, tourists and pleasure-seekers.

The cruise evolution started long before the sun and fun of 'Loveboat,' or the opulence of 'Titanic'. Passenger shipping got its start aboard commercial vessels dedicated to speedy cargo and mail delivery. Itineraries were determined by trade routes and ocean crossings. Ships provided basic transportation for those who sailed out of necessity, immigrants, merchants and the most intrepid of travelers.

High Seas Rivalry and the Need for Speed.

The stakes were high as German Hamburg Amerika and British North American Royal Mail (Cunard) raced each other for the coveted Blue Riband; the award for the fastest transatlantic crossing. Competition for the title of 'Fastest', 'Largest' or 'Most Extravagant' kicked into high gear.

European and North American trade flourished and shipping magnates who had excelled in cargo and mail delivery competed for new customers; passengers who sailed to flaunt their wealth or to flee economic and political repression. A high seas holiday promised first class luxury for the elite; and the promise of an "ocean cure" for body and heart aches. Second-class passengers made do with minimal accommodations and emigrants in steerage held on to high hopes for a new start.

Trans-ocean passenger shipping in the early 1900's was led by Cunard, French Line, Hamburg Amerika Line, Holland America Line, North German Lloyd, , Canadian Pacific, Red Star Line and P. & O.

While most of the cruise evolution took place in the Atlantic, the eastward voyages of the Peninsular and Oriental Steam Navigation Company, P & O, laid the groundwork for exotic cruises to Australia, China, Greece, India, Japan, Palestine and Turkey.

A Sack of Mail or Mrs. Whelan?

When she waved good-bye to her Irish homeland, feisty Mrs. Bessie Whelan weighed in at a petite 150 pounds. The sack of mail bound for America? 150 pounds.

Mail transport was a cut-and-dried, money-making proposition.

But carrying Mrs. Whelan to America required more square footage than a sack of mail occupied; plus such necessities as food, water and toilet facilities. And with Bessie, came that vocal Whelan clan, such as they were. What's a shipping magnate to do?

The Whelans were willing to do anything to insure their passage from impoverished Ireland. Many of their fellow emigrants paid hefty fees and worked as deckhands, janitors and waitresses. For those in steerage, this was not a pleasure cruise.

In 1908, Holland America Line's Rotterdam VI carried 520 first-class, 555 second-class and 2,500 emigrants in steerage. U.S. Congressional uproar over crowded conditions in steerage prompted legislation outlining minimum space per passenger.

A decline in the number of emigrants due to tightening immigration restrictions prompted the industry to court the emerging leisure market with even greater vigor; thus accommodations, facilities, food and service improved.

Rival lines competed with each other and land-based resorts to meet expectations of the moneyed traveler. This passenger demanded five-star accommodations, superior service and sophisticated dining. Luxury liners provided the first class experience expected along with an added splash of high seas adventure.

Extravagant floating playgrounds gained favor with the elite from both sides of the pond, as well-to-do Europeans and American debutantes set sail. Young American tourists also took to the seas: 'roughing it' on transatlantic crossings in steerage became a fashionable and affordable adventure.

Guests began to expect private bathrooms, barber shops, steam heat, enhanced service and gourmet dining. White Star Line's Oceanic (White Star also owned the Titanic) set new standards with a breathtaking grand ballroom 'amidships', larger cabins with in-room water and heat, and steward service.

In 1908, Holland America Line's Rotterdam VI became the first air-conditioned ship. In 1914, the world watched enviously as well-to-do passengers aboard Cunard's Aquitania were invited for a swim in the first shipboard indoor swimming pool.

FIRSTS

1840 The Britania was the first to take passengers on regularly scheduled transatlantic departures. (Operated by the British and North American Royal Mail Steam Packet Company later to become Cunard.)

1873 Holland America Line first formed as the Netherlands-American Steam Navigation Company.

1881 Cunard Servia is the first passenger ship to be lit by electricity.

1908 Holland America Line's Rotterdam VI first fully air conditioned ship.

1911 Cunard's Franconia offers the first shipboard gymnasium and health center.

1912 Hamburg-Amerika Line Victoria Louise begins year-round cruising (Winters in Caribbean.)

1914 Cunard's Aquitania invites guests to swim in the first shipboard indoor swimming pool.

The Caribbean cruise got its start, prior to World War I, with retired transatlantic ships, which were refurbished and redeployed. Active transatlantic liners were also pulled off bitter winter crossings and repositioned on southerly routes. Some of the first cruises and cruise excursions were offered by North German Lloyd, Hamburg Amerika and North American Royal Mail (Cunard.)

World War I interrupted: ocean liners and passenger ships were conscripted for troop transport. In the 1930's, middle-class American pleasure seekers left Prohibition dockside and boarded "booze cruises" to Nassau, Palm Beach, Miami and Havana.

The end of World War II saw ships filled with emigrants and returning military. Postwar prosperity encouraged mass-market ship travel offering new luxuries such as outdoor swimming pools.

Jilted by the Jet Set

The arrival of jet air travel, in 1958, hastened the decline of ship travel. Why chug across the Atlantic in five days when you can fly?! Regularly scheduled transatlantic service dropped off as cargo delivery, transportation and travel shifted to the airlines. In the 1960's and 1970's the golden age of the ocean liner came to an end, and the new age of compact "cruise ships" set sail.

They don't make 'em like they used to.

New and improved engineering and architecture plus Safety of Life at Sea (SOLAS), regulations have sent many oldies but goodies into retirement. The majority of retired ships made their debut before 1970. Some took their final voyage due to an Act of God, others found work as car ferries, converted private yachts or floating casino hotels.

Tips for Older Ships

She's well-preserved, say ship buffs; but before you set sail on a classic older ship, consider her age and performance history. Have technical or mechanical problems been remedied? Like any vehicle, newer ships have fewer problems than those built 25 years ago. Still, for true aficionados, there's nothing like a well-maintained classic.

From One Ship to the World's Largest Cruise LIne

Miami-based Carnival Cruise Lines got its start in 1972 with one ship, the Mardi Gras, formerly the Empress of Canada. 1984 marked the start of the company's network television campaign which enthusiastically introduced Carnival Cruise Lines to the general public. Three new SuperLiners the Holiday, Jubilee and Celebration launched a new 'big is better' design trend that continues throughout the industry.

My, how Carnival has grown! With 15 ships currently in its fleet and 7 newbuilds on order, Carnival Cruise Lines is now the largest cruise line in the world, based on passengers carried. Carnival Corporation and the alliance of the World's Leading Cruise Lines is made up of Holland America Line, Cunard, Seabourn Cruise Line, Costa Cruises and Windstar Cruises.

PART 7

Cruise Line Profiles

Want the Best for Less? Looking for the Perfect Cruise? Cruise Chooser's practical guide to cruise line 'personalities' makes it easy! You'll find answers to these questions:

- ◆ Will there be people like me onboard?
- ◆ Will there be singles, couples and families?
- ◆ Where can I go?
- ◆ When can I travel?
- ◆ What ships are in each fleet?
- ◆ How big are the ships? (size in tons) How many passengers? (capacity)

PLUS:

- ◆ Signature personality traits of major cruise lines.
- ◆ Hallmark programs, facilities, features.
- ◆ NEW Web Sites for discounts and itineraries.
- ◆ NEW Cruise Lines! NEW Ships!

Note: We've profiled major cruise lines. Visit us at **www.cruisechooser.com** for lines not listed here.

Alaska's Glacier Bay Tours & Cruises

[http://www.glacierbaytours.com]
Alaska's Glacier Bay Tours & Cruises is a native-owned Alaskan cruise line specializing in adventure cruises and wilderness tours. These exclusive small ship cruises allow adventurers the unique opportunity to explore Alaska up close. Use the ship as your 'base camp' and enjoy hiking, kayaking, Mendenhall River rafting, visits to a Tlingit Indian village, whale watching in Frederick Sound and searches for grizzlies.

Cruise Areas
Alaska

The Fleet	Capacity
Wilderness Adventurer	74
Wilderness Explorer	36
Executive Explorer	49
Wilderness Discoverer	86

American Classic Voyages Co.

[http://www.deltaqueen.com]
American Classic Voyages Co., AMCV, is the largest owner and operator of US-flag passenger vessels with several lines under its umbrella: the renewed United States Lines, American Hawaii Cruises, The Delta Queen Steamboat Co. and Delta Queen Coastal Cruises.

AMCV's 'Project America' promises a new age of American ship building. The two newbuilds of the United States Lines will be the largest US cruise ships ever built and the first large US-built cruise ships in more than 40 years.

See American Hawaii Cruises, Delta Queen
Steamboat Co., Delta Queen Coastal Cruise, United
States Lines.

Newbuilds

Name	Estimated Delivery Date	Size/Capacity
Project America #1	2003	1,900
Project America #2	2004	1,900

American Hawaii Cruises

[http://www.cruisehawaii.com]
American Hawaii Cruises offers an authentic Hawaiian
experience with year-round cruises aboard its ship,
the ss Independence. Seven-night cruises depart from
Honolulu to visit five ports on four islands. The line's
shore excursions were recognized with Travel Holiday's
'Best of the Best' award. Experience Old Hawaii as the
ship's 'kumu' (teacher) share stories of the fire goddess while you sail past active volcano Mt. Kilauea.
American Hawaii is popular with first-time Hawaii
visitors, mature travelers, golfers, honeymooners and
families with children. Children under the age of 17
sail free (paying only port charges) when sharing
selected cabins with two full-fare adults.

Cruise Areas & Seasons
Year-round: Hawaii

The Fleet	Size	Capacity
SS Independence	30,090	867

American West Steamboat
[http://www.columbiarivercruise.com/]
Visit the historic routes of Lewis and Clark and the
Oregon Trail aboard authentic stern- and paddle-
wheelers. Narrated shore excursions on 4 and 7-
night riverboat cruises introduce guests to the history, culture and scenery of the Pacific Northwest.
Enjoy live, showboat variety entertainment with
musical themes including Country and Western,
Riverboat Jazz, Golden Oldies and Big Band.

Cruise Area & Seasons
Columbia River, Snake River and Willamette River

The Fleet	Capacity
Empress of the North	
Queen of the West	163

Bergen Line, Inc.
(Norwegian Coastal Voyages)
[http://www.bergenline.com]
Bergen Line, Inc. is the US marketing company for
Norwegian Coastal Voyages, whose 11 ships sail the
scenic west coast of Norway year-round carrying
cargo and passengers between Bergen and Kirkenes.
Norwegian Coastal Voyages appeals to passengers
aged 50+, and special interest groups in search of an
in-depth cultural experience. Highlights include
Norwegian art and culture theme cruises and Whale
Safari excursions.

Cruise Areas & Seasons
Year-round: Norway

244

The Fleet	Size	Capacity
Harald Jarl	2,620	164
Kong Harald	11,200	490
Lofoten	2,597	213
Midnatsol	5,205	328
Narvik	4,073	312
Nordkapp	11,350	490
Nordlys	11,200	482
Nordnorge	11,384	464
Polarlys	12,000	479
Richard With	11,200	490
Vesteralen	4,073	318

Canyon Ranch at Sea

Health, Healing and Adventure! The world's first floating health resort, Canyon Ranch at Sea, will dedicate an entire ship to the spa experience; featuring massage and treatment rooms, dance, yoga and excercise studios, sensational pools and even a rock-climbing wall
The Quest I and Quest II offer hight staff-to-guest ratios: 320 guests will be pampered by a staff of more than 300; including 120 spa, health and beauty professionals. Highlights: 90% of oceanview suites will have private verandas.

Newbuilds

Name	Estimated Delivery Date	Size/Capacity
Quest I	2002	320
Quest II	2002	320

Carnival Cruise Lines

[http://www.carnival.com]
Known for its festive-yet-casual atmosphere, Carnival offers a variety of on-board dining, entertainment and activity options for all ages. The 'Most Popular Cruise Line,' is the largest in the world, based on number of passengers carried. The Fun Ships sail on voyages of three to 16 days.

Carnival breaks new ground with 28 different short cruise itineraries from nine different North American homeports - Miami, Tampa, Los Angeles, New York, Galveston, Boston, Charleston, Newport News and Port Canaveral, FL. Highlights: Vacation Guarantee, fantastic casinos, smoke-free Paradise.

Carnival Cruise Lines is a member of the World's Leading Cruise Lines alliance which also includes Holland America Line, Cunard, Seabourn Cruise Line, Costa Cruises and Windstar Cruises.

Cruise Areas & Seasons

Seasonal: Alaska, Hawaii, Panama Canal, Canadian Maritime Provinces, Bermuda
Year-round: Caribbean, Mexican Riviera, Bahamas

The Fleet	Size	Capacity
Celebration	47,262	1,486
Carnival Destiny	101,353	2,642
Ecstasy	70,367	2,040
Elation	70,367	2,040
Fantasy	70,367	2,040
Fascination	70,367	2,040
Holiday	46,052	1,452

Imagination	70,367	2,040
Inspiration	70,367	2,040
Jubilee	47,262	1,486
Paradise	70,367	2,040
Sensation	70,367	2,040
Carnival Triumph	102,000	2,578
Tropicale	36,674	1,022
Carnival Victory	102,000	2,758

Newbuilds

Name	Estimated Delivery Date	Size/Capacity
Carnival Spirit	early 2001	84,000/2,112
Carnival Pride	late 2001	84,000/2,112
Carnival Legend	2002	84,000/2,112
Carnival Conquest	fall 2002	102,000/2,758
Carnival Glory	mid 2003	102,000/2,758
Carnival Valor	fall 2004	102,000/2,758
Carnival Miracle	mid 2003	102,000/2,758

Celebrity Cruises

[http://www.celebrity-cruises.com]
Celebrity Cruises' port-intensive worldwide itineraries attract an international guest list of 85 percent American and 15 percent international travelers. Celebrity appeals to families, couples, honeymooners and singles. Guests range in age from 35-60, with a median of 48 years . Most hold professional/managerial positions, and have household incomes of $60,000 +.
The line is one of two cruise brands owned and operated by Royal Caribbean Cruises Ltd., which also

operates Royal Caribbean International. Highlights: The Millennium at 91,000 gross tons, is the first of four millennium class newbuilds and will be the largest liner to transit the Panama Canal. This new class of ships is 30% larger but the passenger count only increases 8%.

Cruise Areas

Seasonal: Alaska, Caribbean, Bermuda, Bahamas, Panama Canal, Mexico, Europe, Mediterranean, Western Canada, South America

The Fleet	Size	Capacity
Century	70,606	1,750
Galaxy	77,713	1,870
Horizon	46,811	1,354
Mercury	77,713	1,870
Zenith	47,255	1,375
Millennium	91,000	1,950

Newbuilds

Name	Estimated Delivery Date	Size/Capacity
Celebrity Infinity	spring 2001	91,000/1,950
Celebrity Summit	fall 2001	91,000/1,950
Millennium Class	spring 2002	91,000/1,950

Clipper Cruise Line

[http://www.clippercruise.com/]
Clipper Cruise Line's intimate ships bring travelers to secluded waterways and seldom-visited beaches. Zodiac landing craft allow for shoreside exploration of locales larger ships never see. Clipper combines a

high level of comfort and unique itineraries including the Orinoco River, 'Yachtsman's Caribbean,' Far East and South Pacific. Highlights: The captain and his officers maintain an open-bridge policy, allowing passengers to drop in anytime. The lifestyle onboard is casual and unregimented, with an intimate ambiance conducive to camaraderie. Naturalists, historians and other experts offer informal lectures, lead expeditions and invite questions.

Cruise Areas & Seasons
Caribbean, Greenland, High Canadian Arctic, Central and South America, Antarctica, Far East, Pacific

The Fleet	Size	Capacity
Yorktown Clipper		138
Clipper Adventurer		122
Nantucket Clipper		100
Clipper Odyssey		128

Commodore Cruise Line
[http://www.commodorecruise.com]
Commodore offers casual cruising to popular ports at affordable rates. Big Band, Singles, Jazz theme cruises appeal to travelers in their mid 30s to early 60s with middle to upper-middle incomes.

Cruise Areas & Seasons
Year-round: Caribbean, Mexico
Select sailings: Honduras, Mexico, Key West

The Fleet	Size	Capacity
Enchanted Isle	23,395	725
Enchanted Capri	15,410	525

249

Costa Cruises

[http://wwwcostacruises.com]
Costa's international fleet of six ships spans the globe offering cruises of seven-nights and longer. Founded in 1948, Costa is known for its distinctive 'Cruising Italian Style' hospitality. Costa was voted one of the top ten cruise lines by *Travel and Leisure* readers; and voted 'Head of the Class' and 'Top Value Index' by Cruise Reports.

Costa appeals to honeymooners, families and mature travelers. Caribbean cruisers are 35+ with a household income of $50,000+, European cruise travelers are 35+ with a household income of $75,000, college educated, well-traveled and destination oriented. Highlights include the 'Golf Academy at Sea' program, hosted by a PGA-member golf instructor on Caribbean Cruises.

Cruise Areas

Caribbean, Canary Islands, Russia, Fjords, Baltic, North Cape, Mediterranean, Transatlantic

The Fleet	Size	Capacity
CostaAlegra	28,500	820
CostaClassica	53,000	1,308
CostaMarina	25,500	776
CostaRiviera	30,400	974
CostaRomantica	53,000	1,356
CostaVictoria	76,000	1,928
CostaAtlantica	84,000	2,112

Newbuilds

Name	Estimated Delivery Date	Size/Capacity
Unnamed	Sum. 2003	84,0000/2,154
Unnamed	2003	105,000
Unnamed	2004	105,000

Crown Cruise Line

Departures from Aruba, personal attention and moderate prices make the Crown Dynasty a great vacation value. Crown Cruise Line appeals to travelers in their mid 30s to early 60s with middle to upper-middle incomes. A full children's program is available summer and holidays.

Cruise Areas

Caribbean

The Fleet	Size	Capacity
Crown Dynasty	20,000	800

Cruise West

[http://www.cruisewest.com/]
Cruise West provides 'casual, up-close cruising with a personal touch aboard their fleet of small ships. Transit the locks of the Columbia and Snake River dams that make inland voyages possible. Ask your captain to stop the ship to give you a closer look at a bear on shore; he'll even shut down the engines so you can listen to the eagles cry and "crackling glacier ice." Enjoy fresh regional cuisine served in a casual

atmosphere and friendly service from an expert staff. Highlights: Shore excursions to Mt. St. Helens Volcanic National Monument, guest speakers such as Linda Russell , a balladeer whose appearances include Carnegie Hall and A Prairie Home Companion; Phil George, a Nez Perce tribal elder; Junius Rochester, a third generation member of a Washington State pioneer family.

Cruise Areas
Columbia & Snake Rivers, Coastal Canada, Alaska, Pacific Coast, Sea of Cortes, Mexico.

The Fleet	Capacity
Spirit of '98	96
Spirit of Endeavor	102
Spirit of Glacier Bay	52
Spirit of Alaska	78
Spirit of Columbia	78
Spirit of Discovery	84
Sheltered Seas	70

Crystal Cruises
[http://www.crystalcruises.com]
Crystal Cruises received awards for 'World's Best Cruise Line,' and 'World's Best Cruise Ship' from *Travel & Leisure* readers survey and 'Best Large Ship Line' from *Conde Nast Traveler* readers' survey. Crystal guests are primarily 35+ with a median age of 64. Most are married, upscale, discriminating travelers. Approximately 85 percent are from the US and Canada; 15 percent are international.
Highlights: Caesar's Palace at Sea casino, Italian and

Asian alternative restaurants, Callaway Golf partnership. Theme cruises include: Crystal Wine & Food Festival, Health & Fitness/Alternative Medicine, Best of Broadway, Computer University @ Sea, Big Band.

Cruise Areas & Seasons
Spring: Panama Canal/Caribbean, Mexican Riviera, World Cruise, Mediterranean
Summer: Alaska/Canada, Western Europe, Baltic, North Cape, British Isles, Mediterranean
Fall: Panama Canal/Caribbean, Black Sea, Mediterranean, Red Sea, Asia, Australia, New Zealand
Winter: Panama Canal/Caribbean, South America, World Cruise
Holiday: South America, South Pacific

The Fleet	Size	Capacity
Crystal Harmony	49,400	940
Crystal Symphony	51,044	940

Newbuilds

Name	Estimated Delivery Date	Size/Capacity
Unnamed	fall 2003	68,000/1,080

Cunard
[http://www.cunardline.com]
With 160 years of classic British heritage, Cunard offers authentic British service and far-reaching itineraries. 'The Queen Mary Project' will introduce a new class of 'grand dame' ships in the tradition of the classic Queen Mary, Queen Elizabeth and QEII. This newest 'World's Larges' will be longer than three

football fields or four city blocks!
Cunard Line Limited operates Cunard and Seabourn
Cruise Line; members of the exclusive World's
Leading Cruise Lines alliance, which includes
Carnival Cruise Lines, Holland America Line, Costa
Cruises and Windstar Cruises.

Cruising Areas & Seasons
Summer: Mediterranean, New England, Bermuda,
Northern Europe, Ireland/Scotland, Transatlantic.
Spring: South Pacific, Panama Canal, Caribbean,
Orient, Colonial South, Transatlantic, World Cruise.
Winter: Caribbean, Asia, Australia, World Cruises,
Panama Canal, South Pacific.
Fall: Africa, Mediterranean, New England, Caribbean,
Adriatic, South America, Arabia, Transatlantic
Christmas Holiday: Panama Canal, Arabia, Caribbean

The Fleet	Size	Capacity
Queen Elizabeth 2	70,327	1,715
Caronia (fka Vistafjord)	24,492	665

Newbuilds Name	Est Delivery Date	Size/Cap
The Queen Mary II	2003	110,000/2620

Delta Queen Coastal Cruises
[http://www.deltaqueen.com]
Beginning in 2001, Delta Queen Coastal Cruises will
offer cruise vacations on specially designed 226-pas-
senger ships along the East and West Coasts of the

United States, the Caribbean and Mexico. Parent company is American Classic Voyages Co.

Cruise Areas & Seasons
US East and West Coastal cruises, Caribbean, Mexico

Newbuilds

Name	Estimated Delivery Date	Size/Capacity
Cape May Light	2001	tba/226
Cape Cod Light	2001	tba/226

Delta Queen Steamboat Company
[http://www.deltaqueen.com]
The Delta Queen Steamboat Company provides overnight paddlewheel steamboat vacations with an old-fashioned, American theme. Its three vessels, the Delta Queen, Mississippi Queen, and the American Queen, cruise the US inland waterways on 3- to 16-night excursions.
The Columbia Queen offers eight-night Pacific Northwest cruise vacations.
Parent company is American Classic Voyages Co.

Cruise Areas & Seasons
US inland waterways, Pacific Northwest

The Fleet	Capacity
American Queen	420
Delta Queen	174
Mississippi Queen	414
Columbia Queen	161

Disney Cruise Line

[http://www.disneycruise.com]

Disney defines the 'seamless' vacation from start to finish. Guests are greeted by a Disney representatives at Orlando International Airport; where a custom-designed motorcoach takes you to one of nine Walt Disney World Resort hotels.

Check into your hotel and you're registered for the entire vacation, both ship and shore. Enjoy three or four days of unlimited admission to theme parks, water parks and entertainment districts and hop another Disney motorcoach to meet your ship at the Disney art deco terminal at Port Canaveral, Florida.

Highlights: Both ships feature staterooms 25% larger than the industry average, original Broadway-style entertainment and extensive children's programming-with an entire deck devoted to kids. 'Rotation dining' gives guests an opportunity to experience a different dining atmosphere nightly - while receiving continuing personal attention from the same waiter. Disney is not just for kids - and adult-only restaurant provides a private getaway.

Disney now offers three-, four- and seven-day cruises

Cruise Areas & Seasons

Year-round: Nassau and Castaway Cay.

The Fleet	Size	Capacity
Disney Magic	83,000	1,750
Disney Wonder	83,000	1,750

First European Cruises (Festival Cruises)
[http://www.first-european.com]
First European's new flagship, Mistral, attracts a cosmopolitan guest list: her inaugural hosted cruisers from more than 25 nations, including France, Austria, Belgium, Germany, Italy, Spain, Switzerland, UK, Australia, Brazil, China, Peru and the US.
First European Cruises ' departures from Guadeloupe and port-intensive European cruises appeal to upper-middle and middle-class experienced cruisers, ages 30 to 70. Highlights: Shopping aboard the Mistral is made easy for all nationalities - the Euro has been chosen as the official onboard currency. First European/Festival Cruises is operated by P & O.

Cruise Areas & Seasons
Winter: Canary Islands, Caribbean
Spring & Fall: Egypt/Israel, Turkey/Black Sea, Italy, Spain, Western Mediterranean
including Morocco, Tunisia and West Africa
Summer: Greek Islands, Turkey, Scandinavian Fjords, Baltic Sea

The Fleet	Size	Capacity
Azur	14,717	720
Bolero	16,107	802
Flamenco	17,042	784
Mistral	47,900	1,200

Newbuilds

Name	Estimated Delivery Date	Size/Capacity
European Vision	Sum. 2001	1,400
European Dream	2002	1,400

Holland America Line

[http://www.hollandamerica.com]

Holland America Line offers premium cruises to more than 250 destinations worldwide including popular Alaskan voyages and new Hawaiian itineraries. Winner of the 'Best Value in Cruising ' award from the World Ocean & Cruise Liner society for the last seven years.

Now in its 53rd year in Alaska, Holland America's voyages feature an on-board naturalist to help guests better understand and appreciate the geography, geology, biology and ecology of the 'Last Frontier.' HAL's seven-day Glacier Bay Inside Passage cruises feature 30 hours of port time during visits to Juneau, Skagway and Ketchikan, in addition to a nine-hour cruise the full length of Glacier Bay National Park. HAL's "Great Land Tour" of Alaska was designated an official American Pathways 2000 itinerary, part of the White House Millennium Trails initiative. The tour includes meetings with the Haida people of Ketchikan's rain forest and the Inupiat Eskimo of Kotzebue.

Highlights: Club HAL children's activity program, exclusive children's shore excursions, Passport to Fitness activity program, 'tipping not required,' 'Flagship Forum' cultural lecture series, gentleman social hosts on all sailings of 14 days and longer.

Cruise Areas & Seasons

Spring: Mexico, Hawaii, Trans-Atlantic, Pacific Coast, Panama Canal, Caribbean, Far East/Orient, Southeast Asia
Summer: Alaska, Europe, Mediterranean,

Scandinavia, Russia, New England, Canada,
Caribbean
Fall: Mexico, Hawaii, Trans-Atlantic, Pacific Coast,
Panama Canal, South America, New
England/Canada, Caribbean
Winter: Southeast Asia, Africa, Far East/Orient,
Australia, Grand World Voyage, Panama Canal,
Caribbean
Winter: Spring & Fall: Panama Canal

The Fleet	Size	Capacity
Amsterdam	61,000	1,380
Maasdam	55,451	1,266
Noordam	33,930	1,214
Rotterdam	59,652	1,316
Ryndam	55,451	1,266
Statendam	55,451	1,266
Veendam	55,451	1,266
Westerdam	53,872	1,494
Volendam	65,000	1,440
Zaandam	65,000	1,440

Newbuilds

Name	Estimated Delivery Date	Size/Capacity
New Class	fall 2002	1,800
New Class	sum. 2003	1,800
New Class	2003	1,800
New Class	2004	1,800
New Class	2005	1,800

Lindblad Expeditions

[http://www.expeditions.com]
Lindblad Expeditions' shallow-draft ships and flexible itineraries bring you up close to wildlife and cultural sites. Hop a Zodiac landing craft and explore any-where, anytime- on a moment's notice. 30 to 110 guests receive personal attention and expert answers from highly qualified naturalists and historians. Highlights: All-inclusive rates, informal talks about destinations and unassigned dining, high staff to guest ratio.

Cruising Areas & Seasons

Africa, Alaska, Antarctica, Baja California, Caribbean; Central, North and South America; Egypt, Galapagos, Middle East, Pacific Northwest, Transatlantic

The Fleet	Capacity
Sea Lion	70
Sea Bird	70
Polaris	80
Caledonian Star	110
Swedish Islander	49

Mediterranean Shipping Cruises

[http://www.msc.cruisesusa.com]
Mediterranean Shipping Cruises offers unique European itineraries on smaller ships appealing to couples, families and honeymooners from their mid-40's to 70's. Mediterranean Shipping Cruises' varied fleet carries from fewer than 100 fellow passengers to more than 2,600 guests. Set sail on cruise ships, sail-assisted cruise vessels, or a paddle-wheel riverboat.

Cruise Areas & Seasons

Winter: Caribbean, South America, South Africa
Spring, Summer & Fall: Sicily, Tunisia, Spain, France,
Greek Islands, Egypt, Israel, Portugal, Malta, Black
Sea, Lebanon, Syria, Italy

The Fleet	Size	Capacity
Melody	36,500	1,072
Monterey	20,040	550
Rhapsody	16,495	760
Symphony	16,852	760

Norwegian Cruise Line

[http://www.ncl.com]
As one of the world's largest lines, NCL offers more
than 100 cruise itineraries, ranging from three to 23
days, and calls at over 200 destinations. NCL attracts
families, active singles and young professionals 25-49,
and special interest groups.
Cruise the Norwegian Way with Broadway shows,
Sports Afloat®, Dive In™ snorkeling, dining choices... plus a great Kid's Crew™ program.
NCL Holding ASA is the parent company of
Norwegian Cruise Line, Orient Lines
and Norwegian Capricorn Line an Australia-based
line catering to the Spanish cruise market. Star
Cruises holds a controlling interest in NCL.

Cruise Areas & Seasons

Fall: Canada/New England
Winter: South America
Summer & Fall: Mediterranean
Spring, Summer & Fall: Alaska, Europe, Bermuda,

Hawaii
Year-round: Bahamas, Caribbean, Mexico
Repositioning: Panama Canal, Transatlantic

The Fleet	Size	Capacity
Norway	76,049	2,032
Norwegian Dream	50,760	1,748
Norwegian Majesty	38,000	1,460
Norwegian Sea	42,000	1,510
Norwegian Sky	80,000	2,002
Norwegian Wind	50,760	1,748

Newbuilds

Name	Est. Delivery Date	Size/Capacity
Norwegian Sun	fall, 2001	80,000/2,000
Norwegian Sky-class	April, 2002	80,000/2,000
SuperStar Libra-class	fall, 2002	2,300

Orient Lines

[http://www.orientlines.com]
A specialist in destinational cruising, Orient Lines has been awarded 'Best itineraries' and 'Best Value' by the World Ocean & Cruise Liner Society. Cruises are five to 27 days with guest lecturers and gentlemen hosts featured on long voyages.
Orient Lines appeals to travelers 35+ seeking value-oriented cruise vacations with a destinational/educational focus, four-star comforts and excellent service. Exotic itineraries attract passengers 55+. Orient Lines is owned and operated by Norwegian Cruise Lines.

Cruise Areas & Seasons

Spring: India/Egypt, Southeast Asia
Fall: Egypt/Africa
Winter: Australia, New Zealand, Java Sea, Antarctica
Spring, Summer & Fall: Mediterranean/Greek Isles

The Fleet	Size	Capacity
Marco Polo	22,080	850
Crown Odyssey	34,250	1,050

P & O

[http://www.pocruises/]
Traveling to more than 180 destinations in 75 countries, P & O draws on its heritage as a pioneer of
cruising to offer delightful British-style holidays. The
parent company of Princess Cruises, P & O, Peninsular and Oriental Steamship Company, began in
1840 with routes to Egypt and India and by 1845,
P & O's regular steamer service reached Malay and
China. The line's world-class superliner Aurora
sports a 30-foot high waterfall, wrap-around promenade deck and three pools; one with a terraced
design, one with a sliding glass roof and another just
for families. P & O also operates First European/
Festival Cruises.

Cruising Areas

World Cruise, Panama Canal, Mexican Riviera, South
Pacific, Asia, Egypt, India

The Fleet	Capacity
Arcadia	1,620
Aurora	1,878

Oriana	1,810
Victoria	745

Cruise Areas & Seasons
Atlantic, Baltic, Caribbean, Mediterranean,
Norwegian Fjords & Iceland, World Cruises

Newbuilds

Name	Estimated Delivery Date	Size/Capacity
Unnamed	2004	2,600

Princess Cruises
[http://www.princesscruises.com]
One of the 'Big Four,' Princess Cruises' popular 'Love Boats' visit 220 ports worldwide on voyages of seven to 65 days. Princess Cruises appeals to first-timers and experienced travelers including young couples, families and mature cruisers. The line currently carries 620,000 passengers annually; and with its newest ships will cater to cater to more than one million guests by 2001. Signature award-winning vacations are Princess' Alaska Cruisetours; 10-day Northern European voyages and the 72-day world cruise, which visits 26 ports on six continents
Highlights: Hearts & Minds wedding chapel, Love Boat Kids™ children's program. Recognition by the gastronomic society Chaine des Rotisseurs has been awarded to the entire Princess fleet. Princess passengers: check your mailbox for savings certificates enclosed in the quarterly Captain's Circle News.

Cruise Areas & Seasons
Spring: Bermuda, Caribbean, Hawaii/Tahiti, Holy
Land, Mexico, Orient/Asia, Panama Canal, South
America, South Pacific
Summer: Alaska, Europe
Fall: Australia/New Zealand, Caribbean, Hawaii/Tahiti,
Holy Land, Mexico, Orient/Asia, Panama Canal,
South America
Winter: Africa/India, Australia/New Zealand,
Caribbean, Mexico, Panama Canal, South America
also: World Cruise

The Fleet	**Size**	**Capacity**
Crown Princess	70,000	1,590
Dawn Princess	77,000	1,950
Grand Princess	109,000	2,600
Pacific Princess	20,000	640
Regal Princess	70,000	1,590
Royal Princess	45,000	1,200
Sea Princess	77,000	1950
Sky Princess	46,000	1,200
Sun Princess	77,000	1,950
Ocean Princess	77,000	1,950

Newbuilds

Name	**Estimated Delivery Date**	**Size/Capacity**
Golden Princess	5/2001	109,000/2,600
Star Princess	3/2002	109,000/2,600
Coral Princess	fall 2002	88,000/1,950
Island Princess	2003	88,000/1,950
Diamond Princess	2003	110,000/2,600
Sapphire Princess	2004	110,000/2,600

Radisson Seven Seas Cruises

[http://www.rssc.com]

This fleet of distinctive luxury ships; including the catamaran styled Radisson Diamond; travels to 500 destinations worldwide. Radisson Seven Seas Cruises attracts experienced cruisers, age 45 to 50+, well-educated, with household incomes of $100,000+. Highlights: Aboard the trend-setting Seven Seas Navigator, every stateroom is a suite with its own private balcony. Royal Music Festival, PGA Golf cruises in Europe, Asia and the Caribbean.

Cruise Areas & Seasons

Winter: Antarctica, Australia, New Zealand, Caribbean, Indonesia, Panama Canal &   Costa Rica, Vietnam, China, Hong Kong, Singapore
Spring: Arabia, Baltic, Caribbean, Europe, India, Mediterranean, North Cape, Panama Canal, Costa Rica
Summer: Alaska, Baltic, Europe
Fall: Antarctica, Arabia, Caribbean, Central and South America, India, Mediterranean, Panama Canal, Costa Rica, Vietnam, Singapore, Hong Kong
Year-round: Tahiti, French Polynesia

The Fleet	Size	Capacity
Hanseatic	9,000	184
Paul Gauguin	18,800	320
Radisson Diamond	20,295	350
Seven Seas Navigator	30,000	490
Song of Flower	8,282	180

Newbuilds

Name	Estimated Delivery Date	Size/Capacity
Seven Seas Mariner	2/2001	46,000/720

Regal Cruises

[http://www.regalcruises.com]
Affordable vacations aboard the classic Regal
Empress range in length from one-to three-night
Sunspree Party cruises to 12 night voyages through
the Canadian Fjords. The Regal Empress sails sea-
sonally from Port Manatee, FL (Tampa Bay),
Philadelphia, Mobile, New York, and Savannah.
Theme cruises include Country & Western, Big Band,
and Oldies. Regal Cruises is popular with both repeat
and first-time cruisers of all ages.

Cruise Areas & Seasons

Winter & Spring:(from Port Manatee, FL,
Philadelphia & Mobile, AL)
Caribbean, Costa Rica, Colombia, Mexico, Panama,
Grand Cayman, Key West, New Orleans
Summer & Fall: (from New York & Savannah),
Bahamas, Caribbean, Canada, New England,
Newfoundland, South America

The Fleet	Capacity
Regal Empress	875

ResidenSea Ltd.

The newest concept in cruising, World of ResidenSea will set sail spring 2001 on a three year fixed itinerary of world cruises. Residents will choose from 110 'apartments' ranging from 1,100 square feet to 3,200 square feet in size, plus their choice of six floor plans including penthouses and bi-level residences. These two or three bedrooms units will have a fully equipped kitchen; private terrace with whirlpool; walk-in closets; personal computer and 24-hour security.

88 additional guest suites will range from 220 to 500 square feet in size. Decor includes custom furnishings, linen, china, cutlery and crystal. See Trends in Cruising.

Cruising Areas
World-wide

Newbuilds

Name	Estimated Delivery Date	Size/Capacity
World of Residensea	2002	40,000 tons

Renaissance Cruises
[http://www.RenaissanceCruises.com]
Renaissance offers destination intensive itineraries, open seating in every dining room, and an all-adult, smoke-free environment. The Renaissance fleet consists of two distinct product lines. 'R-Class' ships R1 through R6 each carry 684 guests on 11-16 day vacations. The all-suite Renaissance VII and Renaissance VIII accommodate 114 passengers. CruiseTours include free round-trip air; European packages also include free 2-6 night deluxe hotel stays.

Cruising Areas
Asia, Africa, Greek Isles, Mediterranean, South Pacific

The Fleet	Capacity
R1	684
R2	684
R3	684
R4	684
R5	684
R6	684
Renaissance VII	114
Renaissance VIII	114

Royal Caribbean International
[http://www.royalcaribbean.com]
One of the 'Big Four,' Royal Caribbean International appeals to couples and singles age 30-50, and families. With worldwide itineraries and an expanding fleet of profitable ships, Royal Caribbean affordable cruise vacations give active travelers high value and variety.

Highlights: RCI's Royal Journeys program offers Explore Overnight excursion where guests may leave the vessel, spend one to three nights at an alternative destination and then rejoin the ship in another port-of-call. The Voyager of the Seas boasts a 900-seat arena with broadcast facilities and recreational facilities that include a rock climbing wall, in-line skating rink, golf course and regulation-sized sports court; a wedding chapel and the cruise industry's largest conference area.

Royal Caribbean Cruises Ltd., is a global cruise company operating two cruise brands, Royal Caribbean International and Celebrity Cruises.

Cruise Areas & Seasons

Summer: Mediterranean, Scandinavia/Russia/Norwegian Fjords, Europe
Fall: Mexican Riviera, New England
Summer & Fall: Alaska, Bermuda, Transatlantic, Hawaii
Fall & Winter: Europe, Middle East, Australia & New Zealand
Winter, Fall & Spring: Panama Canal
Year-round: Bahamas, Caribbean, Baja Mexico

The Fleet	Size	Capacity
Enchantment of the Seas	74,140	1,950
Explorer of the Seas	74,140	1,950
Grandeur of the Seas	74,140	1,950
Legend of the Seas	69,130	1,800
Majesty of the Seas	73,941	2,350
Monarch of the Seas	73,941	2,350
Nordic Empress	48,563	1,600
Rhapsody of the Seas	78,491	2,600
Sovereign of the Seas	73,192	2,250
Splendour of the Seas	69,130	1,800
Viking Serenade	40,132	1,500
Vision of the Seas	78,491	2,000
Voyager of the Seas	142,000	3,114

Newbuilds Name	Estimated Delivery Date	Size/Capacity
Radiance of the Seas	2001	2,000
Adventure of the Seas	fall 2001	3,100

Brilliance of the Seas	2002	2,000
4th Voyager-class	2002	3,100
5th Voyager-class	2003	3,100
3rd Vantage-class	2003	2,000
4th Vantage-class	2004	2,000

Royal Olympic Cruises

[http://www.royalolympiccruises.com]
Royal Olympic Cruises upholds the traditions of predecessors Sun Line and Epirotiki; and is the largest cruise line in the Greek Isles. Specializing in a more personal, culturally-enriching vacation experience, the line features destination-oriented itineraries with an extensive 'World Affairs' ambassador lecturer series including winter soft-adventure cruises to South America and the 'Land of the Maya.' Royal Olympic appeals to experienced travelers, ages 40-70, affluent and college-educated, who prefer cultural, destination-focused itineraries.

Cruise Areas & Seasons

Spring, Summer & Fall: Greek Isles, Turkey, Holy Land, Egypt and Black Sea
Winter: Amazon River/Carnival in Rio, Land of the Maya, Panama Canal, circumnavigation of South America, Orninoco River.

The Fleet

The Fleet	Size	Capacity
Odysseus	12,000	400
Olympic Countess	18,000	840
Orpheus	6,000	280
Stella Oceanis	5,500	300

Stella Solaris	18,000	620
Triton	14,000	620
World Renaissance	12,000	457
Olympic Voyager	25,000	840

Newbuilds

Name	Estimated Delivery Date	Size/Capacity
Olympic Explorer	2001	25,000/ 840

St. Lawrence Cruise Lines

[http://www.stlawrencecruiselines.com/]
Enjoy early 1900's decor, private shore excursions,
afternoon tea and nightly entertainment as you
cruise the sheltered waters of canals and locks.
All-inclusive calm water cruises include tours, entertainment, accommodations and generous home-
quality meals. More than 95 percent of Canadian
Empress passengers are 55 and older, some retired
with married couples in the majority. (50 percent
American, 34 percent Canadian, 16 percent British
and European.)

Cruise Areas & Seasons
Canadian Coast and Rivers

The Fleet
Canadian Empress

Seabourn Cruise Line

[http://www.seabourn.com]

Seabourn appeals to affluent cruisers 45+ who are accustomed to top-grade hotels and resorts, First Class air travel and fine dining. The line also appeals to first-time cruisers. With voyages ranging from 4 to 99 days, Seabourn's itineraries and exceptional shore excursions take you worldwide. Cruise up the Chang Jiang River and explore ancient palaces or take a moonlit Amazon River safari in a dugout canoe! Enjoy gourmet single-seating dining, elegant restaurants and casual dining. Seabourn is operated by Cunard Line Ltd., and is a Carnival family member.

Cruise Areas

Asia, Arabia, India, Europe, European Rivers, Mediterranean, North America, Russia, Scandinavia, South America, Trans-Oceanic cruises, including transatlantic, transpacific voyages; and World Cruise.

The Fleet	Size	Capacity
Seabourn Sun (fka Royal Viking Sun)	37,845	758
Seabourn Goddess I (fka Sea Goddess I)	4,250	116
Seabourn Goddess II (fka Sea Goddess II)	4,250	116
Seabourn Pride	10,000	208
Seabourn Legend	10,000	208
Seabourn Spirit	10,000	208

Sea Cloud Cruises

[http://www.seacloud.com]

Sailing yachts and River vessels

Enjoy smooth passage aboard the carefully restored classic 1931 sailing yacht, Sea Cloud. Four masts, brilliant white sails, rich mahogany and gleaming brass promise an authentic cruise experience. River vessel River Cloud, offers cruises through heart of Europe: the Rhine, Main, Moselle, and Danube. Sea Cloud's newest tall ship, the 96-passenger Sea Cloud II will cruise in Northern Europe, taking her five-star service to the Mediterranean and South America.

The Fleet	Capacity
Sea Cloud	70
River Cloud	

Newbuilds Name	Estimated Delivery Date	Size/Capacity
Sea Cloud II	2000	96
River Cloud II	2000	

Silversea Cruises

[http://www.silversea.com]
Silversea's yacht-like vessels cater to only 296 guests with spacious surroundings, all-suite accommodations and all-inclusive rates. The line attracts discriminating guests accustomed to plush accommodations and individual service. Highlights: The 'Silver Links Golf Series' gives guests an opportunity to play as many as seven full rounds of golf in five countries within 12 days.

Conde Nast Traveler Reader's Choice Awards named Silversea the 'World's #1 vacation choice' 1996, and 'World's Best Small Cruise Line' *Travel & Leisure's* Reader's Choice Awards 'World's Best Small Cruise Line'

Cruise Areas
Mediterranean, Northern Europe, Baltic, Far East, Canada, Colonial America, Australia, New Zealand, South Pacific, Africa, India, Panama Canal, Mexican Riviera, Amazon, South America.

The Fleet	Size	Capacity
Silver Cloud	16,800	296
Silver Wind	16,800	296
Silver Shadow	25,000	388

Newbuilds Name	Estimated Delivery Date	Size/Capacity
Silver Whisper	7/2001	25,000/388

Star Clippers
[http://www.starclippers.com/]
All three ships in the Star Clippers fleet are sail-powered, like the 19th Century clipper ships, except much larger, and fitted out luxuriously in mega-yacht fashion. While the fleet has the most modern navigational and ship handling gear, they are operated in traditional fashion, with equipment proven by years at sea. Highlights: Sail the Mediterranean aboard the Royal Clipper, the world's largest true sail ship.

Cruise Areas
Year-round: Caribbean, Mediterranean
Summer: Greek Islands
Winter: Indonesia

The Fleet	Capacity
Star Flyer	170
Star Clipper	170
Royal Clipper	228

Star Cruises
[http://www.starcruises.com]
'The Leading Cruise Line in Asia-Pacific' appeals to international tourists with fly/cruise packages from Australia, Japan, Europe, Korea, Taiwan, China and South East Asia.

Star Cruises is one of the four largest cruise lines in the world and by year 2005, will have a fleet of 12 vessels sailing from Singapore, Port Klang, Phuket, Bangkok, Hong Kong, Taipei and Osaka/Kobe. Star Cruises made its debut in September, 1993, and has captured 70% of the cruise market in Asia-Pacific, carrying more than 1 million passengers during in the first 5 years. The company plans to market its new vessels more to Europe, the Middle East and the US. Star Cruises holds a controlling interest in Norwegian Cruise Line.

Cruise Areas
South Korea, Taiwan, Hong Kong, Singapore, Vietnam, Thailand, China, Malaysia.

The Fleet

	Capacity
Star Aquarius	1,900
Star Pisces	2,192
SuperStar Aries	678
SuperStar Gemini	900
SuperStar Leo	2,800
SuperStar Virgo	2,800
MegaStar Aries	72
MegaStar Taurus	72
SuperStar Taurus	950

Newbuilds

Name	Estimated Delivery Date	Size/Capacity
SuperStar Libra	2001	91,000/2256
SuperStar Scorpio	2002	91,000
SuperStar Sagittarius II	2004	112,000/2998
SuperStar Capricorn II	2005	112,000/2998

United States Lines

[http://www.unitedstateslines.com]
'American-owned, American-crewed and American-built '

A new fleet cruise ships is now being developed under the American Classic Voyages Company's Project America initiative. The original United States Lines' ships, such as the ss America, ss Manhattan, ss Leviathan and ss George Washington, were the favorites of a glamorous passenger list that included the Duke and Duchess of Windsor, 'Tennessee' Williams, Cary Grant and Salvador Dali. In 1969,

United States Lines' last remaining passenger vessel, the fabled ss United States withdrawn from service.

The company's three ship fleet will be joined by two 1,900-passenger, 72,000 grt cruise ships - the first major, ocean-going passenger ships to be built in the US in more than 40 years.

Cruise Areas & Seasons
Hawaiian Islands

The Fleet	Size	Capacity
Patriot (fka Nieuw Amsterdam)		1,214

Newbuilds

Name	Estimated Delivery Date	Size/Capacity
TBA	2003	72,000/1,900
TBA	2004	72,000/1,900

Victoria Cruises
[http://www.victoriacruises.com]
The only cruise line sailing the entire navigable length of the majestic Yangtze River. Experience ancient wonders on 3-10 day cruises aboard comfortable modern ships. Victoria's western cruise directors introduce you to Chinese heritage and culture with lectures, demonstrations, shore excursions and entertainment.

Cruise Areas & Seasons
Yangtze River, China

The Fleet	Capacity
Victoria I	154
Victoria II	154
Victoria II	154
Victoria IV	154
Victoria Princess	158
Victoria Pearl	158
Victoria Blue Whale	160
Victoria Angel	154

Windstar Cruises
[http://www.windstarcruises.com]
Known for its luxury cruise experience, superb cuisine and casual dress code, Windstar Cruises operates three identical 148-passenger sail cruise ships and one 312-passenger sail cruiser. Windstar passengers range in age from 20 to 70, with an average age of 48; and an average income of $75,000 to $200,000. They are mostly professionals, experienced travelers and first-time cruises.

Cruise Areas & Seasons
Fall, Winter & Spring: Caribbean, Costa Rica, Virgin Islands, Panama Canal, Belize
Spring, Summer & Fall: Caribbean, Mediterranean (Greek Isles, Amalfi Coast, Dalmatian Coast, French and Italian Rivieras, Rome, Venice, Spain, Portugal, Provence and Andalusia)

The Fleet	Size	Capacity
Wind Song	5,350	148
Wind Spirit	5,350	148
Wind Star	5,350	148
Wind Surf	14,745	312

Note: We've profiled major cruise lines. Visit us at

www.cruisechooser.com for lines not listed here.

PART 8

Cruise Chooser

CYBERGUIDE
to Money-Saving Web Sites

Get the Best for Less with our easy guide to
cruise Web sites. Listings are alphabetical.
We've done the homework for you!
For more money-saving Web sites visit

www.cruisechooser.com

A

ASSOCIATIONS

American Society of Travel Agents (ASTA)
[http://www.astanet.com]

Association of Retail Travel Agents (ARTA)
[http://www.artahdq.com]

Cruise Lines International Association (CLIA)
[http://www.cruising.org]

Institute of Certified Travel Agents (ICTA)
[http://www.icta.com]

International Council of Cruise Lines
[http://www.iccl.org]

National Association of Cruise Oriented Agents
[http://www.nacoa.com]

AUCTIONS

[http://www.adventurebid.com]

[http://www.bid4vacations.com]

[http://www.etauction.com]

[http://www.onsale.com]

[http://www.travelbids.com]

AIRLINES

Air Canada
   [http://www. aircanada.com]

American
   [http://www.americanair.com]

British Airways
   [http://www.british-airways.com]

Continental
   [http://www.flycontinental .com]

Delta
   [http://www.delta-air.com]

Northwest
   [http://www.nwa.com]

Reno Air
   [http://www.renoair.com]

Southwest
   [http://www.iflyswa.com]

United
[http://www.ual.com]

US Airways
[http://www.usair.com]

B

BOOK STORES

Adventurous Traveler Bookstore
[http://www.adventuroustraveler.com]

Travel Book
[http://www.travelbook.com]

C

CRUISING

[http://www.cybercruises.com]

[http://www.maritimematters.com]

[http://www.compuserve.com] (cruise forum)

[http://www.aol.com] keyword: cruise critic

[http://www.cruisematic.com]

CRUISE LINES

Major worldwide cruise lines and tour operators offering cruise vacations.

Abercrombie & Kent
[http://www.abercrombiekent.com]

Alaska' Glacier Bay Tours & Cruises
   [http://www.glacierbaytours.com]

American Canadian Caribbean Line
   [http://www.accl-smallships.com]

American Cruise Lines
   [http://www.americancruiselines.com]

American Hawaii Cruises
   [http://www.cruisehawaii.com]

American Safari Cruises
   [http://www.amsafari.com]

American West Steamboat co.
   [http://www.columbiarivercruise.com]

Aqua Safaris Worldwide
   [http://www.aqua-safaris.com]

Bergen Line
   [http://www.bergenline.com]

Canodros
[http://www.canodros.com]

Cape Canaveral Cruise Line
[http://www.capecanaveralcruise.com]

Celebrity Cruises
[http://www.celebrity-cruises.com]

Classical Cruises
[http://classicalcruises.com]

Clipper Cruise Line
[http://www.clippercruise.com]

Club Med
[http://www.clubmed.com]

Commodore Cruise Line
[http://www.commodorecruise.com]

Continental Waterways
[http://www.continentalwaterways.com]

Costa Cruises
[http://www.costacruises.com]

Crown Cruise Line
[http://www.applevacations.com]

Cruise West
  [http://www.cruisewest.com]

Crystal Cruises
  [http://www.crystalcruises.com]

Cunard
  [http://www.cunardline.com]

Delta Queen Steamboat Co.
  [http:www.deltaqueen.com]

DFDS/Scandinavian Seaways
  [http://www.seaeurope.com]

Disney Cruise Line
  [http://www.disneycruise.com]

Ecoventura/Galapagos Network
  [http://www.ecoventura.com.ec]

Eurocruises Inc.
  [http://www.eurocruise.com]

First European Cruises
  [http://www.first-european.com]

French Country Waterways
[http://www.fcwl.com]

Galapagos Cruises
[http://www.ecuadorable.com]

Global Quest (fka OdessAmerica)
[http://www.globalquesttravel.com]

Golden Sun Cruises
[http://goldensuncruises.com]

Holland America Lines
[http://www.hollandamerica.com]

Imperial Majesty Cruise Line
[http://www.imperialmajesty.com]

Ivaran Lines
[http://www.ivaran.com]

KD River Cruises of Europe
[http://www.rivercruises.com]

Lindblad Expeditions
[http://www.specialexpeditions.com]

Marine Expeditions
[http://www.marineex.com]

Maui-Molokai Sea Cruises
[http://www.mauigateway.com]

Mediterranean Shipping Cruises
[http://www.msccruisesusa.com]

Neckton Diving Cruises
[http://www.nektoncruises.com]

Norwegian Cruise Line
[http://www.ncl.com]

Nubian Nile Cruises
[http://www.nubiannilecruises.com]

Oceanwide Expeditions
[http://www.diveguideint.com/]

Orient Lines
[http://www.orientlines.com]

Peter Deilmann EuropAmerica
[http://www.deilmann-cruises.com]

Prince of Fundy Cruises, Ltd.
[http://www.princeoffundy.com]

Princess Cruises
[http://www.princesscruises.com]

Quark Expeditions
[http://www.quark-expeditions.com]

Radisson Seven Seas Cruises
[http://www.rssc.com]

Regal Cruises
[http://www.regalcruises.com]

Regal China Cruises
[http://www.regalchinacruises.com]

Renaissance Cruises
[http://www.renaissancecruises.com]

Riverbarge Excursion Lines
[http://www.riverbarge.com]

Royal Caribbean International
[http://www.royalcaribbean.com]

Royal Olympic Cruises
[http://www.royalolympiccruises.com]

St. Lawrence Cruise Lines
[http://www.stlawrencecruiselines.com]

Sea Cloud Cruises
[http://www.seacloud.com]

Seabourn Cruise Line
[http://www.seabourn.com]

Silversea Cruises
[http://www.silversea.com]

Small Ship Cruises
[http://www.smallshipcruises.com]

Spice Island Cruises
[http://www.indo.com/cruises]

Spirit Cruises
[http://www.spiritcruises.com]

Star Clippers Cruises
[http://www.starclippers.com]

Star Cruises
[http://www.starcruises.com]

Swan Hellenic
[http://www.swanhellenic.com]

Tall Ship Adventures
[http://www.tallshipadventures.com]

Temptress Cruises
[http://www.temptresscruises.com]

United States Lines
[http://www.unitedstateslines.com]

Victoria Clipper
[http://www.victoriaclipper.com]

Victoria Cruises, Inc.
[http://www.victoriacruises.com]

Viking River Cruises
[http://www.vikingrivercruises.com]

Windjammer Barefoot Cruises
[http://www.windjammer.com]

Windstar Cruises
[http://www.windstarcruises.com]

World Cruise Company
[http://www.worldcruiseco.com]

World Explorer Cruises
[http://www.wecruise.com]

World's Leading Cruise Lines
(Carnival Family of Cruise Lines)
[http://www.leaderships.com]

CUSTOMS

[http://www.customs.ustreas.gov/travel/forms.htm]

D

DESTINATIONS/SHORE EXCURSIONS

Alaska
  [http://www.alaskanet.com]

Bermuda
  [http://www.bermudatourism.org]

Cancun
  [http://www.yucatanweb.com]

Caribbean
  [http://www. caribbeantravel.com]

Great Britain
  [http://www.bta.com]

Great Outdoors Recreation Pages
  [http://www.gorp.com]

Hong Kong
  [http://www.hkta.org]

Israel
  [http://www.infotour.co.il]

Italy
  [http://www.dolcevita.com]

293

Jamaica
   [http://www. jamaicatravel.com]

Middle East
   [http://www.arab.net]

New England
   [http://www.newengland.com]

Singapore
   [http://www. singapore-usa.com]

DOCUMENTATION
(passports, foreign entry requirements, travel
warnings and advisories.)

[http://www.tiac.net/ users/passport /getforms.html]

[http://www.americanpassport.com]

E

ECO-TRAVEL

   [http://www.ecotourism.org]

   [http://www.teleport.com/earthwyz/

F

G

GAY & LESBIAN TRAVEL

RSVP Travel Productions
    [http://www.rsvp.net]

Family Abroad
    [http://www.familyabroad.com]

Skylink Travel
    [http://www.skylinktravel.com]

Out & About
    [http://www.outandabout.com].

H

HEALTH

Dialysis
    [http://www.dialysis-at-sea.com]

Cruise Ship Sanitation: National Center for
Environmental Health.

    [http://www.cdc.gov/nceh/programs/sanit/
    vsp.htm]

Immunizations/Vaccinations

[http://www.cdc.gov/travel/travel.html]

[http://www.tripprep.com/index.html]

[http://www.medaccess.com]

Vegetarian Journeys
[http://www.vegetarianjourneys.com]

Green Earth Travel
[http://www.vegtravel.com]

Vegetarian Travel Board
[http://www.veg.org]

HISTORY

Maritime Matters
[http://www.maritimematters.com]

Ocean Liner Museum
[http://www.oceanliner.org]

HONEYMOONS

[http://www.honeymoons.com]

I-J-K

L

LITERATURE & REPORTING
Wanderlust
   [http://www.salonmagazine.com/wanderlust]

Mungo Park
   [http://www.mungopark.com]

M

MAPS
(ports of embarkation, ports of call)

MapQuest
   [http://www.mapquest.com]

National Geographic Map Machine
   [http://www.nationalgeographic.com]

N-O

P

PUBLICATIONS/NEWS/REVIEWS

Cruise Industry News
   [http://www.cruiseindustrynews.com]

Cruise Observer
[http://www.cruiseobserver.com]
CyberCruises
[http://www.cybercruises.com/forum]

Tourist Guide
[http://www.touristguide.com]

Travelpage.com
[http://www.travelpage.com/]

TravelTips!
[http://www.travltips.com]

Cruise Opinion
[http://www. cruiseopinion.com]

Rough Guides
[http://www.roughguides.com]

Q

R

RESERVATIONS/BARGAINS
For updates to these sites,
visit **www.cruisechooser.com**

[http://www.americanexpress .com/travel]

[http://www.bestfares.com]

[http://travel.epicurious.com/]

[http://www.expedia.com]

[http://www.fieldings.com] Crowsnest Cruise
Forum, Cruise Finder

[http://www.fodors.com]

[http://www.frommers.com]

[http://www.hotcoupons.com]

[http://www.itn.net]

[http://www.mcp.com /frommers]

[http://www.nationalgeographic.com]
Cruise Guide

[http://www.savtraveler.com]

[http://www.travelhound.com]

[http:// www.travelocity.com]

[http://www.travelquest.com]

[http://www.travelweb.com]

[http://www.travelwiz.com]

[http://www.vacation.com]

[http://www.wtgonline.com]

[http://www.ypn.com/ living/travel]

S

SINGLES CRUISES

Outdoor Singles Network
[http:// www.kcd.com/bearstar/osn.html]

The Only Way to Travel
[http:// www.onlywaytotravel.com]

SPECIAL INTERESTS

Computer Cruises
[http://www.geekcruises.com

Martial Arts
[http://www.napma.com]

Nudist Travel
[http://www.skinnydip.com]

Scuba
[http://www.csn. net/rmdc]

T

TRAVEL COMPANIONS

[http:// www.3wave.com/companions]

[http://www.companions2travel.com]

U

V

VIDEOS

[http://www.vacationsonvideo.com/]

[http://destinations.previewtravel.com/
DestGuides/VideoWorld/]

W

WEATHER

[http://www.cnn.com]

[http://www.weather.com]

WEB CAMERAS ('Live' feeds)

Web Cams from Cruiseships.

Princess Cruises' click on "bridge cam."
http://www.princess.com/

NCL click on "bridge cam"
[http://www.ncl.com/html/fleet/00sky_flpg_]

Web Cams: Rivers, Canals, Ports and Harbors.

Bremerhaven, Germany
[http://www.kmu-net.de/seestadt/webcam/]

Cape Town, South Africa
[http://www.kapstadt.de/lifecam.htm]

Halifax Harbour, Nova Scotia
[http://www.brooknorth.com/camsite/]

Juneau, Alaska
[http://www.go2net.org/alaska/juneau/web
cam.html]

Panama Canal, Panama
[http://www.pancanal.com/photo/camera
java.html]
Port Everglades, Florida
[http://www.justsurfit.com/burtandjacks/web
cams/cam1.shtml]

San Diego Bay, California
[http://live.net/sandiego/]

Seattle, Washington
[http://www.seanet.com/Users/lacas/
loftcam.html]

Sydney, Australia
[http://www.x-zone.canon.co.jp/WebView
E/sites/java/sydney_j.htm]

River Thames, London, England
[http://www.livesights.com/cgi-bin/nph
VideoPages.plx?title=live]

Web Cams Miscellaneous locations

[http://www.earthcam.com]

[http://www.camworld.com]

PART 9

Cruise Chooser

RESOURCE GUIDE

Add more dimension to your travels
with cruise guides, destination guides, maps,
travel narratives, cookbooks, newsletters and
magazines. *Also see the Cruise Chooser*
Cyberguide *to cruise Web sites.*

*Note: Titles listed as the '2001 Guide to
Cruises' are often 'Annuals' and are published
as a new edition every year.*

These resources are recommended by Cruise Chooser:

A
Access Cruise, Access Guides

Alaska & Canada's Inside Passage Cruise Tour Guide

Alaska by Cruise Ship : The Complete Guide to the
Alaska Cruise Experience
Vipons, Anne 2000

Alaska: The Cruise Lover's Guide, Grescoe, Paul and
Audrey Grescoe, 1998

The Argonne Anti-Jet Lag Diet, Argonne National
Laboratories, 97 South class Avenue, Argonne, IL
60439   (708) 252- 5575 Free Article Defeating Jet Lag,
Forsyth Travel Library, 9154 West 57th St., Box 2975,
Shawnee Mission, KS 66201 Free, Send SASE (busi-
ness sized)

B
The Bahamas Cruising Guide, Wilson, Matthew,
et al, 1998

Berlitz 2001 Complete Guide to Cruising & Cruise
Ships, Ward, Douglas, 2000, Berlitz Publishing Co.

C
Canada's Yukon and South Central Alaska Cruise
Tour Guide, 1998

Caribbean by Cruise Ship, Vipond, Anne, 1999

Caribbean Ports of Call Eastern and Southern Regions : A Guide for Today Cruise Passengers, Showker, Kay, 1999

Caribbean Ports of Call Northern and Northeastern Regions : A Guide for Today's Cruise Passengers, Showker, Kay 1999

Caribbean Ports of Call Southeastern, Showker, Kay

Caribbean Ports of Call Western Region : A Guide for Today's Cruise Passengers, Showker, Kay 1999

The Case of the Mystery Cruise (The Adventures of Mary Kate and Ashley, #2), Thompson, Carol 1996

The Cheapskate's Guide to Cruises : The Very Best Trips for the Lowest Cost, Tanenbaum, Stephen et al, 1999

Conde Nast Traveler Caribbean Resort and Cruise Ship Finder, Aaron Sugarman (Editor)

Conde Nast Traveler Magazine

Courtney's First Cruise, Lynne, Janice.

Crossing & Cruising : From the Golden Era of Ocean Liners to the Luxury Cruise Ships of Today, Maxtone-Graham, John.

Cruise Reports, Slater, Shirley and Harry Basch, Luisa Frey-Gaynor et al, (973) 605 2442.

Cruise Ship Cookbook, Von Hundertmark, Connie

The Cruise Ship Cookbook : Elegant Meals with Cunard, Sodamin, Rudolph

The Complete Cruise Handbook, Vipond, Anne, et al, 1996

The Complete Idiots Travel Guide to Cruise Vacations 2001, Golden, Fran Wenograd, 2000, Macmillan Travel.

Cruise Hosting, Bravos, Brooke, 1992

Cruise Ships : An Evolution in Design, Dawson, Philip, 2000

Cruising: A Guide to the Cruise Line Industry, Mancini, Marc Ph.D., 1999

Cruising Alaska: A Traveler's Guide to Cruising Alaskan Waters & Discovering the Interior, Ludmer, Larry H. 1999

Cruising the Caribbean: A Passenger's Guide to the Ports of Call, Rapp, Laura and Diane Rapp, 1997

Cruise News, Driscoll, Michael

Cruise Observer, Grizzle, Ralph

Cruise Vacations with Kids, Stapen, Candyce, 1999

D

Development and Growth of the Cruise Industry, Cartwright, Roger and Carolyn Baird, 2000

Dictionary of the Cruise Industry; Terms Used in Cruise Industry Management, Operations, Law, Finance, Marketing, Ship Design and Construction, Israel, Gloria and Laurence Miller, 1999

E

Econoguide '00-'01: Cruises. (Cruising the Caribbean, Mexico, Hawaii, New England, and Alaska) Sandler, Corey 1999

The Essential Little Cruise Book: Secrets from a Cruise Director for a Perfect Cruise Vacation, West, Jim, 1999

Reading List from Clipper Cruises
[http://www.clippercruise.com/books.htm.]

Clipper Cruises and Longitude Books offer you a "recommended reading list" for Clipper voyages. Each list features an essential reading package of four or five books and a map.

Sample: Clipper's Medieval Seaports of Western Europe

Clipper Cruises' Recommended Reading:

Amsterdam: Amsterdam and the Hague
(Art in Focus) Christopher Wright / Hardcover/
Bullfinch Press / Published 1995

Basque Cooking and Lore
Darcy Williamson / Paperback /
Caxton Printers / Published 1991

The Illuminated Manuscripts of Medieval Spain
Mireille Mentre / Hardcover /
Thames & Hudson / Published 1996

*Assault on Normandy: First-Person Accounts
from the Sea Services*
Paul Stillwell (Editor) / Hardcover /
United States Naval Inst. / Published 1994

The Autumn of the Middle Ages
Johan Huizinga, et al / Hardcover /
University of Chicago Press / Published 1996

*D-Day June 6, 1944: The Climactic Battle of
World War II*
Stephen E. Ambrose / Hardcover /
Published 1994

*The Pilgrimage: A Contemporary Quest for
Ancient Wisdom*
Paulo Coelho, Alan Clarke (Translator) /
Paperback / Harper San Francisco /
Published 1995

F

Fielding's Alaska Cruises and the Inside Passage, Slater, Shirley, 1997

Fielding's Guide to Caribbean Cruises, Slater, Shirley, et al, 2001

Fielding's Guide to European Cruises, Slater, Shirley, et al. 2000

Fielding's Worldwide Cruises 2001, Slater, Shirley and Harry Basch, Fielding Worldwide.

Fodor's '01: The Best Cruises, M.T. Schwartzman, Editor. Fodor's Travel Publications.

Fodor's 2001 Alaska Ports of Call, Schwartzman, M. T., Fodor's Travel Publications.

Fodor's 2001 Caribbean Ports of Call, Fodor's Travel Publications.

Fodor's 2001 the Best Cruises, Fodor's Travel Publications.

Fodor's 2001 Europe Ports of Call, Fodor's Travel Publications.

Frommer's 2001 Caribbean Cruises and Ports of Call

Frommer's 2001 Alaska Cruises & Ports of Call, Golden, Fran Wenograd and Jerry Brown

Frommer's Born to Shop Caribbean Ports of Call,
Gershman Suzy, 1997

G
Globetrotter Cruise Guide, Bow, Sandra 1999

Great Cruise Ships and Ocean Liners from 1954 to
1986 : A Photographic Survey, Miller, William H., Jr.
1988

H
Harman's Official Guide to Cruise Ships, Harman,
Jeanne.

Have Grandchildren, Will Travel., Pilot Books

How to Get a Job with a Cruise Line, 5th Edition, Miller,
Mary Fallon, Ticket to Adventure, Inc. 1-800-929-7447

I, J, K, L

M
Mediterranean by Cruise Ship, Vipond, Anne, et al
1998

Modern Cruise Ships, 1965-1990 : A Photographic
Record, Miller, William H., 1992

N, O

P
Passport's Illustrated Guide to Caribbean Cruising,
Stanford, Emma Stanford and Thomas Cook, 2000

R

S

Savvy Crusing, 2001, Maxtone-Graham, John, 2000

Selling the Sea: An Inside Look at the Cruise Industry, Dickinson, Bob and Andy Vladimir

Stern's Guide to the Cruise Vacation 2001, Stern, Steve B., 2000

T

The Total Traveler by Ship, Blum, Ethel, 2000

Travel Agent Guide to Wheelchair Cruise Travel, Cushing, Bill.

Travel Smarts, Getting the Most for your Travel Dollar, Teison, Herbert and Nancy Dunnan, Globe Pequot Press

U

The Unofficial Guide to Cruises 2001, Showker, Kay and Bob Sehlinger, Macmillan Travel.

V

Vegetarian Traveler, Civic, Jed and Susan Civic.

W

Wheels and Waves: A Cruise, Ferry, River, and Canal Barge:Guide for the Physically Handicapped, Aroyan, Genie and George Aroyan

X, Y, Z

PART 10
Cruise Guides

- Cruise Guide for Active Adults

- Cruise Guide for Children

- Cruise Guide Credit Card Acceptance

- Cruise Guide for Honeymooners

- Cruise Guide for On-Board Meeting Facilities

- Cruise Guide for Lean and Light Shipboard Cuisine

- Cruise Guide for On-Board Spa Facilities

- Cruise Guide for Worldwide Destinations

Source: Cruise Lines International Association, CLIA

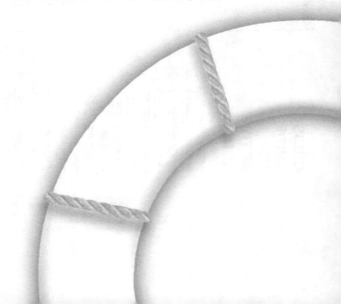

CRUISE CHOOSER

ASHORE*

	BICYCLING	CHARTER FISHING	GOLF	HIKING	HORSEBACK RIDING	SCUBA DIVING	SNORKELING	TENNIS	WATER SKIING	WINDSURFING
AMERICAN CRUISE LINES INC.	A/I	A/I	A/I	A/I	A/I	A/I	A/I	A/I	A/I	A/I
AMERICAN HAWAII CRUISES	–	–	–	I	–	–	–	–	–	–
CAPE CANAVERAL CRUISE LINE	A/I		A/I	A/I	S/I	A/I	A	S		
CARNIVAL CRUISE LINE	–	–	–	–	–	–	–	–	–	–
CELEBRITY CRUISES INC.	–	–	–	–	–	A/I	–	–	–	–
COMMODORE CRUISE LINE	–	S	–	A/I	–	A/I	A/I	S	–	–
COSTA CRUISE LINES	A/I	A/I	S	S	S	S	S	S	S	S
CRYSTAL CRUISES	S	S	A/I	S	I	–	A/I	S	S	S
CUNARD LINE	A	A	S	A	S	A	S	S	S	S
DISNEY CRUISE LINE										
FIRST EUROPEAN CRUISES	S	A	A	S	S	A	A	A	A	A
HOLLAND AMERICA LINE	–	–	–	–	S	–	–	–	–	–
MEDITERRANEAN SHIPPING CRUISES			A				A			
NORWEGIAN COASTAL VOYAGE INC.										
NORWEGIAN CRUISE LINE	–	–	A	–	–	–	A	A	A	A
ORIENT LINES	–	–	–	–	–	–	–	–	–	–
PREMIER CRUISE LINES	S/I	S/I	S/I	S/I	S/I		S/I	S/I	S/I	S/I
PRINCESS CRUISE LINES	S	S	S	S	S	S	S	S	S	S
RADISSON SEVEN SEAS CRUISES	–	–	–	S	–	–	A	–	–	A
REGAL CRUISES	–	–	–	S	–	–	–	–	–	–
ROYAL CARIBBEAN INTERNATIONAL	S	S	S	S	S	S	S	S	–	–
ROYAL OLYMPIC CRUISES	–	–	–	–	–	–	A/I	–	–	–
SEABOURN CRUISE LINE	–	S	A	A	–	A	A/SP	A	A	A/SP
SILVERSEA CRUISES	–	–	–	A	–	–	A/SP	A	A	A/SP
WINDSTAR CRUISES	–	S	–	A	S	–	A/SP	I	A/SP	A/SP

ON-BOARD

	AEROBICS	BASKETBALL	LOW CAL MENU	GOLF DRIVING	GYM	JOGGING	MASSEUSE	PADDLE TENNIS	SAIL BOATING	SAUNA	SCUBA DIVING	SKEET/TRAP SHOOTING	SNORKELING	SNORKELING LESSONS	SPA POOL	SWIMMING	TOTAL FITNESS PROGRAM	VOLLEYBALL	WATER/JET SKIING	WINDSURFING
AMERICAN CRUISE LINES INC.	A		A	A	A	A	A	A	A/I		A/I	A	A/I	A/I		A			A/I	A/I
AMERICAN HAWAII CRUISES			A			A	A	A			–		A			A			–	
CAPE CANAVERAL CRUISE LINE	A		A	A	A	A	A	A		A	A/I	A	A/I	A/I	A	A	A	A	–	–
CARNIVAL CRUISE LINE	S		S		A	A	S	A	–	A	–		A/I	–	A	A	A	A	–	–
CELEBRITY CRUISES INC.	A		A		A	A	A	A		A	S/I	S	A/I	A/I	A	A	A		–	–
COMMODORE CRUISE LINE	A	S	A		A	S	A	S	–	A	S	S	S	S	A	A	A	S	S/SP	S/SP
COSTA CRUISE LINES	A	S	A		A	S	A	A	S	S	–	S	–	–	A	A	A	A	S/SP	S/SP
CRYSTAL CRUISES	A	S	A		A	A	A	A		A		A	S	S	A	A	S			
CUNARD LINE	A	S	A		A	S	A	A		A	–	S	A		A	A	A	A		
DISNEY CRUISE LINE	A		A		A	A	A	A		A			A		A	A	S			
FIRST EUROPEAN CRUISES	A		A		A	A	A	A		A			A		A	A	A	A		
HOLLAND AMERICA LINE	A		A	S	A	A	A	S		S	–		–		A	A	A	S		
MEDITERRANEAN SHIPPING CRUISES		S			A	A	A	S		A					S	A				
NORWEGIAN COASTAL VOYAGE INC.																				
NORWEGIAN CRUISE LINE	A	S	A		A	A	A	A	–	A	–	A	A	A	A	A	A	S		
ORIENT LINES	A		A		A	A	A	A		A			–	–	S	A				
PREMIER CRUISE LINES	A	S/I	A	S/I	S	A	A	S	S/I	S	S	S	S/I	S/I	S/I	A	S	S/I	S/I	S/I
PRINCESS CRUISE LINES	S	S	A	S	S	A	A	A	–	A	–	S	S	S	S	A	A	A	–	–
RADISSON SEVEN SEAS CRUISES	A		A	A	A	A	A	A	–	A	–		A	A	A	A	A		A	A
REGAL CRUISES		S	A		A	A	A	A		A	A		A/I	A/I	A	A		S	–	–
ROYAL CARIBBEAN INTERNATIONAL	A		A		A	A	A	A	A/I	A	A	A	A/I	A/I	A	A	A		A	A
ROYAL OLYMPIC CRUISES	S		A		A	S	S	S	A	S	A/I		S		A/SP	A/SP	A/I		A	A/SP
SEABOURN CRUISE LINE	A		A		A	A	S	A	A	A	–	A	A/SP	–	A	A	A		A	A/SP
SILVERSEA CRUISES	A		A		A	A	A	A	A	A	–		A/SP		A	A	A		A	A/SP
WINDSTAR CRUISES	S		A		A	A	A	A	A/SP	A	A/SP	–	A/SP	A	A	A	S		A/SP	A/SP

CRUISE GUIDE FOR ACTIVE ADULTS

KEY
A–All ships
S–Some ships
I–Information on local facilities provided by shipboard staff
SP–Ship(s) equipped with aft water sports platform

NOTE*
(1) There is an additional charge for most shore-side activities. Some shipboard activities such as skeet-shooting, are also ex
(2) Some water and shore-side sports aren't available in every port or destination (i.e., snorkeling in Alaska)
(3) Unless marked "I", available shore-side activities are provided through shore excursions and sports programs OR arrang
at a passenger's request

CRUISE GUIDE FOR CHILDREN

SPECIAL ACTIVITIES AND SERVICES

Cruise Line	Reduced Cruise Rate (w/ 2 full-fare adults) 1	Air/Sea Rate (same or less for full fare psgrs.)	Babysitting Avail. 2	Cribs Avail. 3	Quad/Family Cabins Available	Arts/Crafts Classes	Basketball	Beach Parties	Bridge Tours	Cartoons	Daily Papers	Dancing Classes	Escorted Shore Tours	Foreign Language Classes	Games/Contests	History/Geography Classes	Ice Cream Bar/Party	Menus	Movies	Parties	Ping Pong	Pool (Just Kids)	Snorkeling	Teen Ctr or Disco	Teen Counselors	Video Games	Volleyball	Youth Ctr/Playroom	Youth Counselors
AMERICAN CRUISE LINES INC.	A			A	A	A			A	A	A		A	A	A	A			A				A						
AMERICAN HAWAII CRUISES	A	A	A	A	A	A		A	A		A	A	A	A	A	A	A	A	A	A	A		A	A	A			A	A
CAPE CANAVERAL CRUISE LINE		A		A	A	A			A	A		S	S		A			A	A	A						A		A	A
CARNIVAL CRUISE LINES	A		A	A	A	A	S			A	A	A			A		A	A	A	A	A	A		S	A	A	A	A	A
CELEBRITY CRUISES INC.	S	A	A/H	S	A	H		S			A/H	S		S	S	S	A	A	A	A	A	S		S	A/H	A	S	A	A/H
COMMODORE CRUISE LINE	A	A		A	A	A	S		S	S	S	S		H	A	H	A	A	A	S	A			A	H	S		S	H
COSTA CRUISE LINES	A	A	A	A	A	A/H	A/H	S	A/H	A	A	A/H		S	A/H	S	A	A	A	A	S	S		S	S	S	S	A	A
CRYSTAL CRUISES	A	A	A	A	T	S	S	S	S/H	A	A/H	S		S	A	S	A	A	A	A/H	A/H			S	A/H	A/H		A	A/H
CUNARD LINE	A	A	A	A	S	A	A	S/H	A	H	S	A	A		A		S	H	A	A	A		S	S	H	S	S	S	H
DISNEY CRUISE LINE	A	A	A	A	A	A	A	A	A	A	A	A	A		A		A	A	A	A		A	A	A	A	A		A	A
FIRST EUROPEAN CRUISES	A	A	A	A	A	A	S	S	A	A	A	A		A	A	A	A	A	A	A	A	A		A	A	A	A	A	A
HOLLAND AMERICA LINE	A	A	A	A	A	A	S	A		A/H	A	S	S	S/H	A	S	A	A	A	A	A	S		A	A	A		A	A
MEDITERRANEAN SHIPPING CRUISES	A		A	A	A					S				S	S			A	S			S		S	S	S	A	S	S
NORWEGIAN COASTAL VOYAGE INC.				S	S/T								A													S		S	
NORWEGIAN CRUISE LINE			A	A	S	S	S	S	S	S	S	S/H	S		H		S	A	S	S	A		S	S/H	A/H	A		S	A/H
ORIENT LINES					A	H		H	H						A				A	H	H				H				H
PREMIER CRUISE LINES	A	A		A	A	S/H	S	S	A/H		A/H	S/H	S	S/H	A	S/H	A	A	S	A	A	S	S	S	S	S	S	S	S/H
PRINCESS CRUISES	A	A	A	A	A	A	S	A	A	A	A/S	A/S		S	A	S	A	S	A/S	A/S	A	S		S	A/S	S	A	S	A/S
RADISSON SEVEN SEAS CRUISES (4)				S	S																								
REGAL CRUISES		A	2	A	A	A			A	A					A			A	A	A	A			A	A	A		A	A
ROYAL CARIBBEAN INTERNATIONAL	S	A	A	A	A	A	S	S	S	A	A		A		A		A	A	A	A	A	S	S	S	A	S	S	S	A
ROYAL OLYMPIC CRUISES	A		2	A	S	S/H			A	S/H	S	A		S	A	S			A	A	A			A	S/H	S		S/H	S/H
SEABOURN CRUISE LINE (4)			A	S			S			H		S	A		A			A	A	A	A				H	S	S	H	H
SILVERSEA CRUISES (4)		A																A	A				S				S		
WINDSTAR CRUISES (4)					T		S												A				S			S	S		

KEY

A = All ships; S—Some ships and/or destinations;
T = No four-berth cabins available, but some triples;
H = Only seasonally; ususally Christmas, Easter and summer holiday periods. Whenever children are aboard, most ships go out of their way to accommodate them and their needs...the more children on a sailing, the greater variety of special activities

(1) On most cruise lines, infants travel free. Where applicable, the maximum age for this rate ranges from 1 to 3 years;
(2) Where available, babysitting is arranged on-board, and not-guaranteed
(3) Where available, cribs arranged for at time of booking;
(4) Children under 12 not encouraged.

CRUISE GUIDE FOR CREDIT CARD ACCEPTANCE

	AMEX			MASTERCARD			VISA			DINERS CLUB			DISCOVER		
	DEPOSITS ONLY	ONBOARD ONLY	EVERYTHING	DEPOSITS ONLY	ONBOARD ONLY	EVERYTHING	DEPOSITS ONLY	ONBOARD ONLY	EVERYTHING	DEPOSITS ONLY	ONBOARD ONLY	EVERYTHING	DEPOSITS ONLY	ONBOARD ONLY	EVERYTHING
AMERICAN CRUISE LINES INC.			•			•			•			•			•
AMERICAN HAWAII CRUISES			•			•			•			•			•
CAPE CANAVERAL CRUISE LINES INC.			•			•			•			•			•
CARNIVAL CRUISE LINES			•			•			•						•
CELEBRITY CRUISES INC.			•			•			•						•
COMMODORE CRUISE LINE			•			•			•						•
COSTA CRUISE LINES			•			•			•			•			•
CRYSTAL CRUISES			•			•			•			•			
CUNARD LINE			•			•			•			•			•
DISNEY CRUISE LINE						•			•						
FIRST EUROPEAN CRUISES			•			•			•			•			•
HOLLAND AMERICA LINE			•			•			•						
MEDITERRANEAN SHIPPING CRUISES						•			•						
NORWEGIAN COASTAL VOYAGE INC.		•				•			•		•				
NORWEGIAN CRUISE LINE			•			•			•			•			•
ORIENT LINES			•			•			•						•
PREMIER CRUISE LINES			•			•			•			•			•
PRINCESS CRUISES			•			•			•			•			
RADISSON SEVEN SEAS CRUISES			•			•			•						•
REGAL CRUISES						•			•			•			•
ROYAL CARIBBEAN INTERNATIONAL			•			•			•						•
ROYAL OLYMPIC CRUISES			•			•			•			•			•
SEABOURN CRUISE LINE			•			•			•		•	•			•
SILVERSEA CRUISES			•			•			•			•			•
WINDSTAR CRUISES			•			•			•			•			•

CRUISE GUIDE FOR HONEY-MOONERS

	SUNDAY/MONDAY DEPARTURES	COMPLIMENTARY CHAMPAGNE/WINE RECEPTION	COMPLIMENTARY CAKE	FLOWERS	TABLE FOR TWO	DOUBLE BED OR EQUIVALENT	SPECIAL AMENITIES
AMERICAN CRUISE LINES INC		●		●	■	●	
AMERICAN HAWAII CRUISES		●	●		●	SC	Wedding/Honeymoon Packages available. Vow Renewal Ceremony on all 7-night cruise. Sunday to Sunday cruise. Hotel Package available.
CAPE CANAVERAL CRUISE LINE	●					●	Wedding/Vow Renewal/Honeymoon Packages available.
CARNIVAL CRUISE LINES	●	●	●		■	■	Honeymoon Group Photo & Party; Wedding & Vow Renewal Ceremonies available.
CELEBRITY CRUISES INC.	●	●	●		●	●	Honeymoon Package available (flowers, bathrobes, champagne, etc).
COMMODORE CRUISE LINE	●	●		●	■	□	Honeymoon & Anniversary Packages available with advance booking.
COSTA CRUISE LINES	●	●	●	●	●	●	Honeymoon Package available. Wedding Program, cabin decorations, honeymooner party certificate.
CRYSTAL CRUISES	■	●		●	■	●	Special amenities are available.
CUNARD LINE	■	●	●	●	●	SC	Cocktail Party.
DISNEY CRUISE LINE	●	●	●	●	■	●	Honeymoon Packages available.
FIRST EUROPEAN CRUISES	●	●	●	●		●	Gift from Captain.
HOLLAND AMERICA LINE	●	●	●	●	●	●	Honeymoon Package available. Vows Renewal Package. Weddings On-Board.
MEDITERRANEAN SHIPPING CRUISES							
NORWEGIAN COASTAL VOYAGE INC.							
NORWEGIAN CRUISE LINE	●	●	●		●	●	Certificate, Photo & Cocktail Party.
ORIENT LINES	●	●	●		●	●	Honeymoon/Anniversary Gift Package available.
PREMIER CRUISE LINES	●	●	□	□	□	□	Honeymoon packages and special amenities available upon request. Cocktail Party, Weddings On-Board.
PRINCESS CRUISES	●	●	●	●	●	●	Honeymoon Packages available which include flowers & champagne in the stateroom.
RADISSON SEVEN SEAS CRUISES	●	●	●	●	●	●	Champagne.
REGAL CRUISES	●	●	●			●	Honeymoon Package available.
ROYAL CARIBBEAN INTERNATIONAL	●	●		●	□	●	Wedding, Vow Renewal & Honeymoon Packages available. Honeymooner party.
ROYAL OLYMPIC CRUISES		●	●	●	■	■	Champagne Toast.
SEABOURN CRUISE LINE	●	●	●	●	●	●	Certificate, Photo.
SILVERSEA CRUISES	●	●	●	●	■	●	All-inclusive luxury.
WINDSTAR CRUISES	●	●	●	●	●	●	Honeymooners' Cocktail Party with Captain on all ships. Gifts for purchase are available.

KEY   □ Available in selected categories/ships   ■ Limited   SC SELECT CABINS

CRUISE GUIDE FOR ON-BOARD MEETING FACILITIES

SPECIAL ACTIVITIES AND SERVICES

	AUDIO CASSETTE PLAYER	COMPUTER EQUIPMENT	CONFERENCE ROOMS	CONFERENCE DINING	CONFERENCE CALLING	DISTRIBUTION	E-MAIL	FAX MACHINE	FLIP CHARTS & EASEL	MEETING COORDINATOR	MICROPHONE	MODEM	OVERHEAD PROJECTOR	PHOTO COPIER	PODIUM	PRINTING	SECRETARIAL SERVICES	SLIDE PROJECTOR	TELEVISION	TRANSLATING SERVICES	VCR	WALKIE TALKIES
AMERICAN CRUISE LINES INC.	A	A	A				A	A	A		A	A	A	A	A			A	A		A	
AMERICAN HAWAII CRUISES	SR	SR	A			A	A	A	A	A	A	A	A	A	A		SR	A	A	SR	A	SR
CAPE CANAVERAL CRUISE LINE	A								SR			A	SR	A	A			A	SR	SR	A	SR
CARNIVAL CRUISE LINES		SR	A	A		SR				A						A		A	A		A	
CELEBRITY CRUISES INC.	A	A	A	A			A		A	A	A	SR	A	A	A	A		A	A	A	A	
COMMODORE CRUISE LINE			A					S	S					S					A		A	
COSTA CRUISE LINES	A		A			A	A	A	A	A	A	A	A	S	A	A	SR	A	A	A	S	SR
CRYSTAL CRUISES	A	A	S	S	S		A	A	A	A	A	A	A	A	A	A	A	A	A	A	A	
CUNARD LINE			A				S	A	A		S		A	A	A	A			S		S	
DISNEY CRUISE LINE		S							A													
FIRST EUROPEAN CRUISES			A						S	SR											SR	SR
HOLLAND AMERICA LINE	SR	SR	A				SR	SR	A		SR	SR	A	A	A	A		SR	A	SR	A	
MEDITERRANEAN SHIPPING CRUISES	SR		A				S	S	A	A	S	S	A	A	A			S	S	A	S	
NORWEGIAN COASTAL VOYAGE INC.																						
NORWEGIAN CRUISE LINE						A	A	A	A	A	A	A	A	A	A		A	A	A		A	SR
ORIENT LINES	A	SR	A					A	A	SR	A	A	A	A	A	A		A	A	A	A	
PREMIER CRUISE LINES	A		A	SR				A	A	A	A	A	A	A	A	A		A	A	A	A	
PRINCESS CRUISES	A	S	A				S	A	A	A	A	A	A	A	A	A	A	A	A	A	A	
RADISSON SEVEN SEAS CRUISES			S						A		A											
REGAL CRUISES	SR	SR	A					A	A	A	A		A	A	A	A		A	A		A	
ROYAL CARIBBEAN INTERNATIONAL	S	S	A				S	A	A	S	A	A	A	A	SR			A	A	A	A	A
ROYAL OLYMPIC CRUISES			A	SR				A	A		A	A	A	A	A	A		A	A	A	A	
SEABOURN CRUISE LINE		A	SR				A		A			A						A	A	A	A	
SILVERSEA CRUISES		A	SR					A	A	A	A	A	A	A	A	A		A	A	A	A	A
WINDSTAR CRUISES		A	SR				A	A	A	A	A	A	A	A	A	A	A	A	A	A	A	A

KEY   A–All ships; S–Some Ships and/or destinations; SR–Special Request

CRUISE GUIDE FOR LEAN & LIGHT SHIPBOARD CUISINE

	LOW CHOL/LOW FAT	LOW SODIUM	SPA PRESCRIBED	DIABETIC	VEGETARIAN	KOSHER	PROGRAM NAME
AMERICAN CRUISE LINES INC.	•	•		SR	SR	SR	
AMERICAN HAWAII CRUISES	•	SR	SR	SR	•	SR	Pu'uwai
CAPE CANAVERAL CRUISE LINE	SR	SR		SR	▲	SR	Diet Conscious Selections
CARNIVAL CRUISE LINES	•	•	•	SR	•		Nautica Spa Selections
CELEBRITY CRUISES INC.	SR	SR		SR	•	SR	Lean & Light
COMMODORE CRUISE LINE	•	•	SR	•	SR	SR	Lite Cuisine
COSTA CRUISE LINES	SR	SR	SR	SR	•	SR	
CRYSTAL CRUISES	•	•	•	SR	•	SR	Lighter Fare
CUNARD LINE	•	•	•	•	•	SR	Spa Cuisine
DISNEY CRUISE LINE	SR	SR		SR	•	SR	TBD
FIRST EUROPEAN CRUISES	•	SR	SR	SR	•	•	
HOLLAND AMERICA LINE	•	SR	•	•	•	SR	Light & Healthy Menu
MEDITERRANEAN SHIPPING CRUISES	SR	SR		SR	SR	SR	Regal Bodies
NORWEGIAN COASTAL VOYAGE INC.	SR	SR		SR	SR		
NORWEGIAN CRUISE LINE	•	•	•	•	•	SR	Lean Entree
ORIENT LINES	•	SR		SR	•	SR	The Lighter Choice
PREMIER CRUISE LINES	SR	SR	SR	SR	SR	SR	SeaFit Cuisine*
PRINCESS CRUISES	•	•	SR	▲	•	SR	Healthy Choice
RADISSON SEVEN SEAS CRUISES	•	SR		SR	SR	SR	Our Light Selection
REGAL CRUISES	SR	SR	SR	SR	•	SR	Heart Line Selections
ROYAL CARIBBEAN INTERNATIONAL	•	SR		▲	•	SR*	ShipShape Menu
ROYAL OLYMPIC CRUISES	•	•	•	SR	SR	SR	Spa Cuisine
SEABOURN CRUISE LINE	•	•	•	SR	•	SR	Simplicity
SILVERSEA CRUISES	•	•	•	SR	SR	SR	Light & Healthy Cuisine
WINDSTAR CRUISES	•	•	•	SR	•	SR	Sail Light Cuisine/ Vegetarian Cuisine

KEY   SR Special Request
         * Must be requested four weeks prior to sailing.
           Kosher foods come in airtight frozen bags. No blessing on-board.
        ▲ On certain items only. (Not full menu)

CRUISE GUIDE FOR ON-BOARD SPA FACILITIES

SPECIAL ACTIVITIES AND SERVICES

	Aroma Spa Body Treatment	Aroma Therapy	Beauty Salon	Body Wrap	Dietician/Nutritionist	Exercise Classes	Exercise Machines	Elemis Synergistic Therapy	Facials	Free Weights	Fitness Evaluations	Heated Mud Therapy	Ionthermie Firming/Toning	Ionthermie Super Detox	Manicures	Massage	Nouveau Vu Health Environment Capsule	Pedicures	Personal Trainer	Reflexology	Saunas	Steambaths	Thalassotherapy	Whirlpools	Workout Wear for Purchase
AMERICAN CRUISE LINES INC.	A		A	A		A	A		A	A					A	A		A							
AMERICAN HAWAII CRUISES		A	A			A	A		A				A		A	A		A							
CAPE CANAVERAL CRUISE LINE	A	A	A	A		A	A		A	A	A	A	A	A	A	A		A	A	A	A	A	A	A	A
CARNIVAL CRUISE LINES	A	A	S	S	A	A	A	A	S	A	A	S	A	A	S	A	A	A	A	A	A	A	A	A	A
CELEBRITY CRUISES INC.	A	A	A	A		A	A	A	A	A	A	A	A	A	A	A	A	A	A	A	A	A	A	A	A
COMMODORE CRUISE LINE	A	A	A	A		A	A	A	A	A	A	S	A	A	A	A		A	A	A	A	A	A	A	A
COSTA CRUISE LINES	A	A	A	A		A	A	A	A	A	A	S	A	A	A	A	A	A	A	A	A	S	A	A	A
CRYSTAL CRUISES	A	A	A	A		A	A	A	A	A	A	S	A	A	A	A	S	A	A	A	A	A	S	A	A
CUNARD LINE	A	A	A	A		A	A	A	A	S	A	A	S	S	A	A	A	A	A	A	S	A	S	S	S
DISNEY CRUISE LINE	A	A	A	A		A	A		A	A	A	A	A	A	A	A		A	A	A	A	A	A	A	A
FIRST EUROPEAN CRUISES						A	A	A	A	A					A	A		A						A	
HOLLAND AMERICA LINE						A	A	A	A	A					A	A		A						A	
MEDITERRANEAN SHIPPING CRUISES						S		A							A										
NORWEGIAN COASTAL VOYAGE INC.																									
NORWEGIAN CRUISE LINE	A		A	A		A	A		A	A	A	A	A	A	A	A		A	A		A	A	A	A	A
ORIENT LINES	A	A	A	A		A	A	A	A	A	A	A	A	A	A	A	A	A	A	A	A	A	A	A	A
PREMIER CRUISE LINES	A		A			A	A	A	A	A	A	A	A	A	A	S	A	A	A	S	A	S	S	A	A
PRINCESS CRUISES	A	A	A	A		S	A	A	A	A			A		S	A	A	S	A	A	A	A		A	A
RADISSON SEVEN SEAS CRUISES	S	A	A	A		A	A	A	A	A	A		A		A	S		A		A	A	A	S	A	A
REGAL CRUISES						A	A		A	A					A	A		A						A	
ROYAL CARIBBEAN INTERNATIONAL	A	A	A	A		A	A	A	A	A	A	A	A	A	A	A	A	A	A	A	A	A		A	A
ROYAL OLYMPIC CRUISES	S	S	A	A		S	S	A	S	S	A		A	A	S	S		S	A	S	A	S		A	A
SEABOURN CRUISE LINE	A	A	A	A		A	A	A	A	A	A	S	A	A	A	A		A	A	A	A	A	S	A	A
SILVERSEA CRUISES	A	A	A	A		A	A	S	A	A	A	S	A	A	A	A		A	A	A	A	A		A	A
WINDSTAR CRUISES	S		A	A	S	A	S	S	S	A	A	S	S	A	S	S		S	A	A	S	A	S	S	S

KEY A–All ships; S–Some Ships and/or destinations

CRUISE GUIDE FOR WORLDWIDE DESTINATIONS

Destination	American Cruise Lines Inc.	American Hawaii Cruises	Cape Canaveral Cruise Line	Carnival Cruise Lines	Celebrity Cruises Inc.	Commodore Cruise Line	Costa Cruise Lines	Crystal Cruises	Cunard Line	Disney Cruise Line	First European Cruises	Holland America Line	Mediterranean Shipping Cruises	Norwegian Coastal Voyage Inc.	Norwegian Cruise Line	Orient Lines	Premier Cruise Lines	Princess Cruises	Radisson Seven Seas Cruises	Regal Cruises	Royal Caribbean International	Royal Olympic Cruises	Seabourn Cruise Line	Silversea Cruises	Windstar Cruises
WORLD CRUISES							•	•				•						•							
WEST COAST				•	•		•	•				•						•							
TRANS-PACIFIC							•	•				•			•			•			•				
TRANS-ATLANTIC				•			•	•			•	•						•	•		•			•	•
SOUTHEAST ASIA							•	•			•	•	•		•	•		•	•		•	•	•	•	•
SOUTH PAC/TAHITI							•	•				•			•			•	•		•				•
SOUTH AMERICA				•	•	•	•	•				•			•			•	•		•		•	•	
SCANDINAVIA				•			•	•		•	•	•		•	•			•	•		•	•	•	•	
RUSSIA/EUROPE				•			•	•		•	•	•		•	•			•	•		•	•	•	•	
RIVER (EUROPE)																								•	
RIVER (CHINA)																								•	
RIVER (AMAZON)				•								•						•					•	•	•
RED SEA/SUEZ CANAL							•	•				•						•			•		•	•	•
PANAMA CANAL				•	•		•	•				•			•			•	•		•	•	•	•	•
NORTH CAPE					•		•	•			•	•	•	•	•			•	•	•	•	•	•	•	•
E. COAST/N. ENG/CAN	•			•	•		•	•				•				•		•	•	•	•		•	•	•
MEXICO				•	•	•	•	•				•			•	•		•	•	•	•	•	•	•	•
MEDITERRANEAN				•			•	•			•	•	•		•	•		•	•		•	•	•	•	•
ISRAEL/EGYPT							•	•			•	•	•		•	•		•	•		•	•	•	•	•
INDIA							•	•				•			•			•	•				•	•	•
IBERIA				•	•		•	•			•	•	•		•			•	•		•	•	•	•	•
HAWAII	•		•				•	•				•			•			•			•		•	•	•
GREEK ISLES/AEGEAN				•			•	•			•	•			•			•			•	•			
FAR EAST/ORIENT							•	•				•			•			•			•	•		•	
EUROPE (EXCL. MED)				•			•	•			•	•			•			•	•		•	•	•	•	•
CRUISES TO NOWHERE								•									•			•			•		
COSTA RICA							•	•				•			•			•			•		•	•	•
CARIBBEAN				•	•	•	•	•		•	•	•	•		•		•	•	•	•	•	•	•	•	•
CANARY ISLANDS/NORTH AFRICA				•	•	•				•	•	•	•		•	•		•	•		•	•		•	•
BRIT ISLES/IRELAND				•	•		•	•				•			•			•	•		•	•		•	•
BLACK SEA				•	•		•	•			•	•			•			•			•	•		•	•
BERMUDA				•			•	•				•						•	•	•	•		•	•	
BALTIC				•			•	•		•	•	•			•			•	•		•	•	•	•	•
BAHAMAS		•	•	•			•	•	•			•			•		•	•		•	•		•	•	•
AUSTRALIA/NEW ZEAL							•	•				•			•			•			•			•	
ALASKA			•	•			•					•			•			•	•		•		•	•	
AFRICA							•	•	•			•			•			•			•		•	•	

INDEX

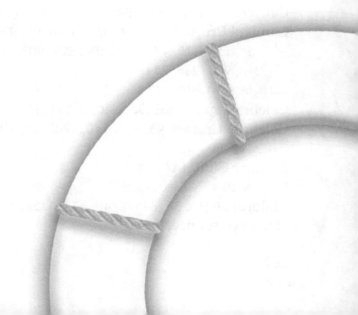

Dear Reader,
Please recommend Cruise Chooser to a friend.
Here is an easy order form.

ORDER FORM   **# of books**_____

Name_____

Address_____

City_____ **State**_____

Zip/Postal _____

Telephone (   ) _____

email _____

Check/Money Order/Visa/Mastercard

Card # _____ _____ _____ _____

exp date _____/_____

Order Now: 1-800-929-7447

outside US   1-727-822-5029

or visit

www.cruisechooser.com

$18.95 + $4 s & h

send check for $22.95
to: Ticket to Adventure
     PO Box 41005
     St. Petersburg, FL
        33743-1005

CRUISE $500 CHOOSER GUARANTEE